What Do I Do If...?

How to Get Out of Real-Life Worst-Case Scenarios

ERIC GRZYMKOWSKI

Adamsmedia
AVON, MASSACHUSETTS

Published by
Adams Media, a division of F+W Media, Inc.
57 Littlefield Street, Avon, MA 02322. U.S.A.
www.adamsmedia.com

ISBN 10: 1-4405-8735-3
ISBN 13: 978-1-4405-8735-1
eISBN 10: 1-4405-8736-1
eISBN 13: 978-1-4405-8736-8

Printed in the United States of America.

10 9 8 7 6 5 4 3 2 1

Library of Congress Cataloging-in-Publication Data

Grzymkowski, Eric.
    What do I do if . . . ? / Eric Grzymkowski.
        pages cm
    Includes index.
    ISBN 978-1-4405-8735-1 (pb) -- ISBN 1-4405-8735-3 (pb) -- ISBN 978-1-4405-8736-8 (ebook) -- ISBN 1-4405-8736-1 (ebook)
    1. Survival. 2. First aid in illness and injury. 3. Home economics. 4. Etiquette. 5. Life skills. I. Title.
    GF86.G79 2015
    613.6--dc23
                            2014046370

This publication is designed to provide accurate and authoritative information with regard to the subject matter covered. It is sold with the understanding that the publisher is not engaged in rendering legal, accounting, or other professional advice. If legal advice or other expert assistance is required, the services of a competent professional person should be sought.

—From a *Declaration of Principles* jointly adopted by a Committee of the American Bar Association and a Committee of Publishers and Associations

Many of the designations used by manufacturers and sellers to distinguish their products are claimed as trademarks. Where those designations appear in this book and F+W Media, Inc. was aware of a trademark claim, the designations have been printed with initial capital letters.

Cover design by Stephanie Hannus.
Cover images © Denise Kappa/123RF; rasslava/123RF; serezniy/123RF; 3drenderings/123RF; Bonzami Emmanuelle/123RF; Denys Semenchenko/123RF; Philip Kinsey/123RF; James Weston/123RF; abirvalg/123RF; Kirill Cherezov/123RF.

This book is available at quantity discounts for bulk purchases.
For information, please call 1-800-289-0963.

Contents

CHAPTER 2: Loss of Limb, Serious Injuries, and Not-So-Serious Injuries — 72

CHAPTER 3: Expensive Mishaps You Wish Had Never Happened — 115

CHAPTER 4: **Obnoxious Hassles and General Pains in the A** — 160**

CHAPTER 5: **Embarrassing Events That Make You Want to Crawl Under a Rock** — **208**

Introduction

Everyone knows that playing dead is the best way to deter a charging grizzly bear, and the only surefire way to dispatch a zombie is a well-placed katana swipe to the head. But do you know what to do when normal, everyday disasters strike?

- How should you handle dropping your fancy smartphone in the toilet?
- Who should you call if a tree falls on your roof?
- What do you do if you have a lingering houseguest?

When the unexpected happens, most people are as poorly equipped to handle food poisoning as they are quicksand—possibly less so—until now.

Fortunately, *What Do I Do If . . . ?* is here to help you solve the far more common, but no less devastating, of life's little curve balls. So whether you're dealing with a tire blowout at 65 mph that makes you suddenly realize, "I have absolutely no idea what I'm supposed to do here," smaller things like losing your ring down the drain, or more serious disasters like being robbed at gunpoint, *What Do I Do If . . . ?* has you covered.

CHAPTER 1

Matters
of
Life and
Death

You don't have to go climb Mount Everest or jump out of an airplane at 30,000 feet in order to face deadly situations. Of the fifteen leading causes of death in the United States, accidents come in at number five, just behind lower respiratory disease.

While you could just stay at home in the fetal position—although there's no guarantee that approach would keep you safe—the far better strategy is to know how to handle yourself, should the unexpected happen.

I've Been Kidnapped

- **Likelihood of Happening:** Low
- **Ease of Prevention:** Moderate
- **Is Time a Factor?** Yes

The idea of a windowless van screeching to a halt and a team of masked assailants pushing you inside may seem absurd, but that doesn't mean it couldn't happen. Although rare, abductions can occur with the hope of ransom, due to cases of mistaken identity, sexual assault, or for no discernible reason at all. But hopefully you won't stick around long enough to find out what your kidnappers have in store for you.

■ Remain Calm and Analytical

Whether you've been kidnapped from your home in the middle of the night or you happened to be the closest person to a bank robber when the police showed up, it's very likely you are scared, nervous, and pumped full of adrenaline. However, if you want to make it out alive, you are going to have to calm down and regain your composure.

Relax your breathing and focus your attention on the details of your surroundings and the situation at hand. Take mental notes of important information like the physical descriptions of your attackers, your current location, any nearby objects you can use to subdue the kidnappers, or anything else you feel might help you escape or apprehend the kidnappers later.

If you are being taken to another location, try to create a mental map of the route you are traveling so you can ascertain approximately where you wind up.

The World's Longest Abduction

On August 4, 1987, a woman dressed as a nurse abducted then nineteen-day-old Carlina Renae White from a New York City hospital, and raised her as Nejdra Nance for twenty-three years. Carlina eventually grew suspicious of her abductor when she was unable to produce important documentation like a birth certificate or social security card. She uncovered the truth by searching missing children databases and discovering photos of herself as an infant.

■ Stay Put or Flee?

Whether you comply with your kidnappers or try to make a break for it will depend heavily on why you've been abducted. If you believe your captors intend to ransom you, then you probably shouldn't risk an escape attempt. Even if your family can't afford to pay the ransom, the police may be able to work with them to pull together the necessary funds for a sting operation. If that's the case, your primary goal will be to comply with any request your captors make and do your best to remain calm throughout the ordeal. Remind yourself that, at least for the moment, your life and relative safety are very valuable to the kidnappers. If, however, you feel your captors intend to kill you once they are done with you, then you will almost certainly want to make every effort to get away.

While you attempt to discover the circumstances of your kidnapping, do your best to remain relaxed and civil with your captors. If you are able to establish a connection with one or more of the kidnappers, they may be less likely to harm you later.

■ Wait for the Opportune Moment

If you have little reason to believe that your abductors have any intention of setting you free, you will have to make it out on your own.

To plan your escape, pay attention to any patterns that might form (especially when your captors come and go), and see if there are any failures in their methods of keeping an eye on you. If you are bound, determine all the different circumstances under which they will remove your bindings, such as to eat, use the bathroom, or at specific times of the day to move around. Analyze your captors for possible weak points. Perhaps one guard is prone to slack off while he's on watch, and has a habit of nodding off during his shift. If one of your captors is particularly sympathetic to you, it's possible you will be able to use that to your advantage and request an unscheduled bathroom break while the others are busy.

While you plan, get to know the layout of the area in which you are being held as much as possible. Are you on the bottom floor or the top floor? Are there windows that might be unlocked or easily broken? If you do find yourself unbound and unwatched for even a moment, your knowledge of the nearest exits could mean the difference between a successful escape and an unsuccessful one.

Be particularly wary of any changes to their behavior that may indicate they are planning to kill you. For example, if they stop attempting to conceal their identities or if they become particularly violent or indifferent toward you, you should get ready to act.

Once you feel the time is right, put your plan into action and be prepared to modify your strategy as circumstances change.

I'm Having a Heart Attack

— **Likelihood of Happening:** Moderate
— **Ease of Prevention:** Moderate
— **Is Time a Factor?** Yes

When you're in good health, you probably pay very little attention to the gentle beating of your heart. Which is a good thing, since your heart beats more than 100,000 times a day and you'd never get anything done otherwise. But you might change your attitude if you realize that the next heartbeat could very well be your last.

■ Know the Signs

When characters in movies suffer a heart attack, they invariably clutch their chest before silently keeling over. While sharp chest pain is usually the first sign people recognize when they are experiencing a heart attack, there are several more subtle indicators:

- Pain that radiates from the chest to the upper back, neck, and left arm
- Dizziness or loss of consciousness
- Shortness of breath
- Nausea
- Sense of impending doom
- Erratic heartbeat

While it's quite common for both men and women to experience those types of warning signs, the symptoms of a heart attack can be more subtle in women. They include:

- Mild chest pain and discomfort
- Stomach pain
- Sweating
- Fatigue

Regardless of your gender, you may experience all, some, or none of these symptoms, so it is important to seek medical attention immediately, even if you are not entirely certain you are suffering a heart attack.

■ Get Help Now

There is a significant risk that you will lose consciousness during a heart attack, so if you are alone it is imperative that you dial 911 and alert the operator of your location as soon as possible. Once you are certain help is on the way, locate a bottle of aspirin and chew one full tablet. Chewing the medication, as opposed to swallowing it, ensures it enters the bloodstream as quickly as possible. The aspirin will help ensure that the clot causing the blockage does not get bigger.

Next, get yourself into a half-seated position on the floor with your knees bent and head and back supported with blankets or pillows. Until help arrives, try to remain calm and breathe normally. If you are able, make sure the door to your home is unlocked so that the paramedics can reach you when they arrive.

■ Minimize Your Risk of a Repeat Attack

Depending on the severity of your heart attack, hospital doctors may provide you with medication or perform open-heart surgery to save your life. While your recovery time will depend on the treatment provided, most patients can return to normal activity anywhere from a few weeks to a few months later. While you may feel tired or weak after you return home, it is important that you gradually begin to move around and perform light household chores to rebuild your strength. However, heavy lifting and strenuous activity should be avoided until your doctor deems it safe.

Once you have suffered a heart attack, you are then at greater risk to experience another episode. You can help minimize that risk by:

- Eating a diet that is low in fat, cholesterol, and sodium
- Exercising regularly
- Maintaining a healthy body weight
- Reducing stress and anxiety
- Quitting smoking

Aside from helping to prevent a future heart attack, taking these steps will also help improve your general health.

There's a Deadly Pandemic

Likelihood of Happening: Low
Ease of Prevention: Low
Is Time a Factor? No

While natural disasters like tornadoes, hurricanes, and earthquakes kill tens of thousands of people each year, none of them can hold a candle to widespread flu outbreaks like H1N1, or even deadlier diseases like cholera and tuberculosis. With death tolls in the billions, microscopic viruses are easily the most dangerous thing known to man. How can you protect yourself?

■ Educate Yourself about the Disease

No two diseases are alike, and how you protect yourself in the event of an outbreak will depend heavily on the particular illness you are dealing with. While some viruses spread easily through the air, others require direct contact with the blood or other bodily fluids of an infected person.

When you hear news that a deadly virus is spreading in your area, research all the available information you can gather about how the disease spreads, what the symptoms are, how it's treated, and what your chances of survival are should you contract it. Do not rely on hearsay and speculation, as misinformation can only make the situation more dangerous. Stick to reliable news outlets and official documents issued by medical professionals.

■ Stay Up to Date on Vaccines

Modern medical science has all but eliminated many of the world's most deadly diseases, and the single greatest contributing factor to that success has been aggressive vaccination programs. While a vaccine is not a 100 percent guarantee that you will not contract the disease, it greatly decreases your risk.

If you are traveling to or live in an area where there is an increased risk of contracting a deadly virus, make sure you are up to date on all the proper vaccines and medications to protect yourself. Many vaccines require frequent booster shots every few years, so do not assume that you are immune simply because you've been vaccinated in the past.

■ Stockpile Supplies

Even if you never contract the disease, during a pandemic there's a significant risk of starvation or dehydration as grocery stores and public works shut down due to widespread panic. While you are still able to safely move around outside, take the opportunity to stock up on nonperishable items like canned goods, dehydrated meals, and plenty of bottled water. Ideally you want to seek out items that do not require any cooking, as your access to gas and electricity may become limited.

Pandemics can last for months, or even years, so you will want to procure as much food as you can adequately store in your home. If the outbreak is short, you can always save your stockpile for another potential emergency. At minimum, you should have at least a two-week supply of food and water for everyone in your household.

■ Stay Indoors and Get Medical Help If Needed

For any infectious disease, the best way to avoid contracting it is to avoid contact with anyone who may have contracted it. Whenever possible, remain inside your home and avoid areas with large groups of people like restaurants, movie theaters, and public transportation. If your employer allows it, consider working from home until the pandemic has subsided.

When you must go outside, wear a protective mask, gloves, and goggles to limit your risk of exposure. Even if the disease is not airborne, the mask and goggles will prevent you from touching a contaminated object and then transferring the virus to your eyes or mouth.

If you begin to exhibit symptoms, immediately call for medical assistance and follow the instructions of medical personnel regarding transportation to the hospital. They may need to send a special unit out to your location to ensure you do not infect anyone on your way to receive treatment.

I'm Attacked by Killer Bees

Likelihood of Happening: Low
Ease of Prevention: Moderate
Is Time a Factor? No

In an attempt to create a new species of bee that could produce larger volumes of honey, Brazilian geneticist and agricultural engineer Warwick E. Kerr crossbred European honeybees with African honeybees in the 1950s. In the decades since, the hyperaggressive result of his experiment—commonly known as killer bees—have made their way up through Central America and currently occupy much of the southern United States.

■ Heed the Warnings

Because it is nearly impossible to tell the difference between a hive of European honeybees and Africanized bees, if you encounter any bee-hive, the list of things you should do is quite short:

• Leave it alone and walk away.

The list of things you shouldn't do, however, is far more extensive:

• Touch, poke, prod, or otherwise disturb the hive
• Yell or make loud noise in the vicinity of a hive
• Spray scented perfume
• Handle or display reflective objects like jewelry
• Wear dark clothing
• Swat at or provoke the bees, even if attacked

While European honeybees are relatively docile, failing to adhere to any of these warnings when dealing with killer bees could trigger a deadly attack.

■ Run Like Your Life Depends on It—Which It Does

While individual Africanized bees may be small, a hive of the insects can contain hundreds of thousands of individual bees, each outfitted with a venomous stinger. If they decide to attack, there's no way you will be able to defend yourself against them. Your only option is to run far and run fast.

While a European honeybee will generally only pursue an intruder up to 50 yards from the hive, Africanized bees have been known to give chase for more than half a mile. If the bees begin to attack, immediately start running. If possible, try to run against the direction the wind is blowing. Your pursuers can fly at a speed of approximately 15 mph, but the wind will help to slow them down slightly.

As you flee, resist the urge to swat at the bees, as this will only serve to agitate them further. Instead, do your best to cover your face with your hands or shirt, provided it does not slow you down. Keep moving until you reach shelter or until you've traveled far enough that the bees are no longer pursuing you.

Water Won't Save You

Many victims of killer bee attacks try to escape the aggressive insects by diving into lakes, pools, or rivers—a strategy that can prove successful against their European cousins. Unfortunately this strategy is ineffective, as the bees simply wait above the water and continue the onslaught when the victim resurfaces.

▨ Deal with the Aftermath

Once you are safely indoors, take a look at your body and determine the severity of the attack. When bees sting, they leave the stinger—as well as part of the abdomen—lodged in the skin. The stingers will continue to pump venom into your system even after they have been separated from the bee's body, so you will want to remove them as soon as possible.

To remove the stingers, scrape an object with a thin, blunt edge like a credit card, knife, or fingernail across your skin and the stinger. This is far safer than using your fingers or tweezers, both of which could squeeze more venom into the body. Do not be alarmed by the sheer volume of stingers, as the average human can survive more than 1,000 stings.

If you worry that you might be allergic to bee stings, seek immediate medical attention. For those who are allergic even a single sting can be fatal.

My Ship Is Sinking

— **Likelihood of Happening:** Low
— **Ease of Prevention:** Low
— **Is Time a Factor?** Yes

Whether you've spent your entire life on boats or you are just out for a short whale-watching tour, the last thing you expect is to wind up floating around the open ocean in a life raft—or worse, outside of one. While the chances that your ship will disappear beneath the waves are slim, it's still a good idea to prepare yourself in case that happens.

■ Take Charge of Your Own Safety

While the captain and crew of the ship will do their best to make sure all of the passengers make it out alive, you are ultimately responsible for your own safety. With that in mind, locate a life jacket and ensure that it is tightly fastened on your body. If you are unsure how it functions, there should be instructions printed directly on the life jacket. Once your life jacket is secured, make sure everyone else in your party is properly outfitted in their own survival equipment. This is especially important for children and the elderly.

Do not go back to your cabin to obtain any personal items, as flooding water could trap you. Instead, head to the deck of the ship and await instructions from the crew. If you are on a large cruise ship, use the stairs and avoid elevators, which could become stuck if the power goes out.

■ Do As You're Told

If you are traveling with an experienced crew, they should all have completed extensive emergency evacuation training. They know the ship better than you do, and you should listen to them if they tell you to do something—even if you disagree.

Many large cruise ships perform regular evacuation drills with passengers, so follow the procedures you've rehearsed if that's the case. If you don't already know what to do, pay close attention to the crew and follow the crowd when you're directed to make a move.

■ Get to a Life Boat

A lifeboat offers you the best chance for survival, as it will keep you out of the water and may also contain food and water to keep you alive should you be out on the open water for an extended period of time. If possible, you will want to get into a lifeboat on the deck, before the lifeboat is lowered into the water. This will prevent you from getting wet, and greatly reduce your risk of hypothermia.

If a lifeboat isn't available, find a life preserver or other flotation device to throw out into the water ahead of you. Stay on the ship as long as possible before jumping, and be careful not to leap on top of other passengers or onto any floating debris. Once you are in the water, look for lifeboats or large debris that might support your weight to get yourself out of the water and reduce the risk of hypothermia.

You Don't Need to Be Freezing to Be Hypothermic

Your body cools much faster in water than it does in air, so the risk of hypothermia is much greater if you are submerged in water or you are unable to dry off once you're out of it. Death can occur in as little as an hour when submerged in 50°F water, and cases of hypothermia have been reported in water as warm as 81°F.

■ Avoid the Sun and Don't Drink Seawater

Whether you are in the relative safety of a lifeboat or floating on top of a dresser in the open ocean, it's important to keep reminding yourself that help is on the way and you will be rescued soon.

If you are at sea for several days, do your best to protect yourself from the harmful rays of the sun, and under no circumstances should you attempt to drink seawater. While it may quench your thirst in the short term, it will ultimately lead to dehydration and eventually death. Instead, ration any food and water you may have with you to give yourself the best chance possible to survive until help arrives.

I Can't Find My Child

— **Likelihood of Happening:** Moderate
— **Ease of Prevention:** Moderate
— **Is Time a Factor?** Yes

Most young animals have a natural instinct to remain close to their parents. Human children, on the other hand, seem to have an innate compulsion to wander off in search of danger. As most seasoned parents will tell you when your first child learns to walk, it's not a matter of *if* you'll lose track of your kid, it's *when*.

◼ Stay Calm and Search Nearby

It can be easy to assume the worst when you turn around and discover your child isn't behind you, but there's a good chance he has not gone far at all. If you take a moment to calmly look around, you may just find your child has begun following the wrong person or has stopped to admire something along your path.

As you look around, call out your child's name in a calm, even tone. If you sound panicked or upset, your child may think you are angry and be reluctant to come out. If your child is prone to spontaneous games of hide and seek, pay special attention to large objects he might use to hide behind or inside.

◼ Alert Security

If you are in a shopping center, theme park, or any other contained location, your first step to being reunited with your child is to alert security that your child is missing. If you were walking in the street or at a playground, immediately call the police and wait for an officer to arrive. Be prepared to provide a detailed description of what your child was wearing, as well as a recent photo, if you have one available.

Whether the search is being conducted by a private security team or a police officer, do your best not to interfere. You should offer any help they may need and be prepared to answer any questions they might have about your child, but do not attempt to take over the search. It may be difficult to stand idly by, but rest assured that everything possible is being done to find your child.

■ Stay in One Place

If you have already designated a meeting place with your child where he should go if you get separated, then head straight there and wait. If you do not have a predetermined spot, then head back to the last place you remember seeing your child and don't venture too far from that area.

Make sure you give the search team your cell phone number and let them know where you'll be waiting. That way, they can contact you the moment they locate your child.

Stranger Danger Is Exaggerated

The most recent study conducted by the U.S. Department of Justice found that only 115 of the 797,500 children abducted in a one-year period were taken by a complete stranger.

■ Make a Plan for Next Time

Once you are reunited with your child, take steps to ensure you are both better prepared if you become separated again.

Whenever you go to a new place, designate an easily recognizable area as the "meetup spot" where your child should go if he gets lost. Instruct your child to only seek out police officers or store employees for help, and consider purchasing a cell phone or walkie-talkie to give to your child so he can easily communicate with you if you get separated.

Before you leave the house, take a picture of your child so you have an up-to-date photo. While this may seem excessive, security personnel will have a much easier time identifying him in a crowd if they have a picture of the clothes your child is wearing.

A Volcano Is about to Erupt

Likelihood of Happening: Low
Ease of Prevention: Low
Is Time a Factor? Yes

The earth is home to approximately 1,500 active volcanoes, and that doesn't even include the vast network of hydrothermal vents—underwater volcanoes that spew superheated water on the ocean floor. Of those active volcanoes, roughly 500 have experienced at least one eruption in modern history. While many eruptions are relatively small, more significant blasts can send deadly gases shooting into the atmosphere and level entire cities in a matter of hours.

◾ Have an Exit Strategy

If you live near (or are vacationing in the vicinity of) an active volcano, you should always keep a hazard-zone map as well as proper evacuation procedures with you at all times. These will provide you with detailed evacuation routes, likely lava flow paths, and other valuable information in the event of an eruption.

Determine whether your home, office, or hotel is located in a danger zone, and plan out multiple options for traveling from your most frequented locations to a safer area. Even if you do not believe you will be in immediate danger, it is still important to plan an escape route in case the lava follows an unexpected path.

■ Stock Up on Essentials

Similar to many other natural disasters, volcano eruptions have the ability to knock out power and other utilities for several days, or even weeks. With that in mind, it's important to have at least a few days' worth of food, water, and toiletries in your home that you can grab at a moment's notice should you need to evacuate.

You should also have a few items unique to a volcano eruption, including a gas mask, goggles, and long-sleeved shirts and pants to protect your skin. You'll want to make sure to have any medications you may need, as well as a small first-aid kit and a battery-powered radio.

■ Listen for Sirens and Stay Tuned to the Radio

Any region prone to volcanic activity will have a network of warning sirens set up throughout the area to alert residents of an impending eruption. If you hear them, immediately turn on your radio or television to determine if you are located in a danger zone and need to evacuate. Most likely, however, you will be advised to remain calm and stay indoors.

Close all doors and windows to protect your home from hot ash and harmful gases. If there's no immediate threat, move your cars into the garage to keep them operable in case you need to evacuate suddenly.

America's Hidden Supervolcano

Wyoming's Yellowstone National Park rests on a magma field estimated to be 50 miles long and 12 miles wide. The last major eruption occurred approximately 640,000 years ago, and scientists speculate that the next one could be 1,000 times more devastating than that of Mount St. Helens in 1980.

■ Get to Higher Ground

Lava tends to flow through low valleys. So if you are stranded outside with no hope of finding shelter, your best bet is to get as high as possible. Due to the danger posed by flying rocks and debris, you will want to try to select a location that also provides you some cover in the form of trees or large rocks you can hide behind. If there is no cover available, crouch down on the ground, turn your back to the volcano, and cover your head with your arms. Once the immediate threat has passed, make your way to shelter as soon as possible to protect yourself from secondary dangers like hot ash and poisonous gases.

I'm Outside During a Flash Flood

Likelihood of Happening: Moderate
Ease of Prevention: Moderate
Is Time a Factor? Yes

Flash floods often occur during or following periods of heavy rain, but they can strike quickly and without warning. While the safest place to be is in the upper floors of a tall building, you may not have that option if you are caught out in the open during a flood. Although a sudden flood can prove lethal, there are steps you can take to ensure you make it out alive.

■ Abandon Your Vehicle

Rising water levels are always dangerous, but the risk of drowning increases exponentially if you are trapped inside a vehicle. The average car can be swept away in as little as two feet of water, so it is imperative that you exit your vehicle as soon as possible. If you wait too long, the pressure differential between the air inside your car and the water pressing against it may also make it difficult to open your doors and escape.

Once outside, slowly walk away from the car with your feet positioned so that you face the direction the current is flowing in. This will allow you to use your legs to cushion yourself if the current sweeps you into any large objects. Next, gradually shuffle yourself away from the path of the water in a diagonal line, one step at a time. As you go, do your best to avoid ingesting any floodwater, which may be contaminated with harmful bacteria.

Water versus Wind

Water traveling at a speed of just 10 mph exerts pressures comparable to wind moving at 270 mph. Even relatively slow floods are still capable of moving large boulders, cars, and other heavy debris.

■ Head for Higher Ground

Now that you have removed yourself from immediate danger, it's time to make your way to a temporary shelter. While it may be tempting to return home, this may not be the safest location if your home is located in a valley or is already surrounded by water. Instead, your goal should be to find a location that is as high in elevation as possible.

If your area is prone to floods, there may be designated shelters available where victims of flooding can seek help. This is your best option, as it will be equipped with food, medication, dry clothes, and sleeping accommodations. If no such shelter exists, or you cannot safely travel to one, look for solid structures located far from any rivers, lakes, or other bodies of water, the higher in elevation, the better. Once you are safely inside, remove any wet clothes and wrap yourself in blankets to keep warm. If you feel the building might be at risk for future flooding, head to the highest floor possible and remain there. If water begins to enter your shelter, proceed onto the roof if necessary.

Under no circumstances should you leave the building and attempt to swim your way to safety. Instead, hang light-colored clothes or blankets from the windows to alert rescue personnel that someone is trapped inside and needs assistance.

If you're unable to find any safe shelter that isn't already surrounded by water, your best bet is to head for a tall hill and wait for help to arrive.

I'm Driving Into a Tornado

- **Likelihood of Happening:** Low
- **Ease of Prevention:** Moderate
- **Is Time a Factor?** Yes

Unless you live in the Midwest's aptly named Tornado Alley, you'd probably be as surprised to see a cyclone forming in the middle of the highway as you would to see a family of emperor penguins. While it's true that tornadoes are rare in most parts of the world, they can still crop up almost anywhere in the world with little or no advance warning.

■ Drive Away—Quickly

A tornado can generally travel anywhere from around 30 mph to 70 mph, so it is unwise to attempt to outrun it in your car. However, if you are able to determine the general direction of the tornado, you may be able to avoid it by driving perpendicular to its path. If you have the option, meteorologists recommend traveling directly right at a 90-degree angle, assuming you are facing toward the direction of the tornado's movement. Traveling to the left is more likely to put you in a region of the storm containing the most large hail and heavy rain.

■ Make Do with What's Close

The ideal place to seek shelter during a tornado is a dedicated underground shelter, or the basement of a structurally sound building. If you can quickly get to either, then immediately abandon your vehicle and make your way inside. Once there, cover your body with a mattress or any padded material, or crouch underneath a sturdy piece of furniture to protect yourself from falling debris.

When you are in the middle of the highway, however, the only cover available may be a nearby ditch. If that is the case, park your car on the side of the road a moderate distance away from where you'll seek shelter, to avoid being crushed if it rolls over. Head toward the lowest ground you can find, and lie flat on your stomach with your hands over the back of your head until the tornado passes. Be sure to avoid any tall trees, bridges, billboards, or other large objects when selecting where to hunker down, as these pose a considerable risk of collapsing on top of you.

■ Stay Put?

Although there is much debate over the issue, it may actually be safer to remain inside your car during a tornado. This is especially true if there is considerable debris flying around outside. If you do opt for this method, make sure that your seat belt is secured and your car is parked on a flat surface with the windows rolled up. Next, lean your head down below the level of the windows and cover yourself with a blanket or jacket, if you have one available. Remain this way until the tornado has passed and you deem it is safe to exit your vehicle.

A Hurricane Is on Its Way

- **Likelihood of Happening:** High
- **Ease of Prevention:** Low
- **Is Time a Factor?** Yes

Every year, the world is subjected to approximately eighty-five significant hurricanes, tropical cyclones, and typhoons. With winds howling in excess of 74 mph and rainfall often measured in feet instead of inches, a single storm can cause millions of dollars of property damage and take the lives of thousands of victims. If you discover your home sits squarely in the hurricane's path, it is not news you should take lightly.

■ Gather Necessities

Unlike tornadoes and earthquakes, which occur without significant warning, hurricanes can often be detected several days before they arrive on land. As a result, you will have ample time to prepare your home for the worst, and possibly even evacuate to a safer location.

In the days leading up to the hurricane, gather up enough canned food and water to last you and your family at least two weeks, and up to a month if you can. While the hurricane won't last that long, you could find yourself without power and unable to leave your home after the storm passes. Freeze any raw meat you may have in your fridge, and fill your freezer to the brim with bottles of water. This will optimize your freezer's efficiency should you lose power.

Make a list of anything you will need to have on hand, and stockpile enough of each item to last at least two weeks, but preferably a month. This includes flashlights, batteries, medications, sanitary products, and anything else you will need on a daily basis.

> ### Bathtubs Make Excellent Troughs
> An average-sized bathtub can hold around 80 gallons of water, which can be used for drinking as well as cooking and cleaning. You can even use the water to flush your toilets, as needed.

■ Hurricane-Proof Your Home

Whether you plan to stay put or evacuate, you want to ensure your home is prepared to weather the storm. Barricade the exterior of all windows either with dedicated storm shutters or wooden planks to prevent flying debris and broken glass from entering the home. This will also deter looters, should riots break out in the aftermath of the storm. Place any lawn furniture, grills, or other outdoor fixtures inside the garage or in the basement.

Inside, move all your furniture, electronics, and other valuables to the topmost floor, and pack any small items in waterproof bags hung from the ceiling.

■ Survive the Storm

When the hurricane does arrive, lock all doors and windows and retreat to the safety of your basement. While there is a risk that the basement could flood, the danger from broken windows and flying debris upstairs is far greater. Be sure to bring along everything you will need for at least twenty-four hours.

If you don't have a basement, or you feel there is significant risk of flash flooding, move to a windowless room in your home large enough to accommodate your entire family, as well as your supplies. This may be a home office, a bathroom, or even a walk-in closet if there are no windowless rooms in your home. Whatever happens, stay far away from any doors or windows until the storm has passed. Keep a battery-powered radio nearby to monitor news of the storm's movements.

Once the winds have died down and authorities have signaled the all clear, you can freely move about your home and assess any damage to the interior and exterior. While it may take some time for the power to return and any floodwater to recede, you should be well prepared to hunker down until things get back to normal.

I'm Stuck in a Rip Current

— **Likelihood of Happening:** Moderate
— **Ease of Prevention:** Low
— **Is Time a Factor?** Yes

From deadly jellyfish the size of your fingernail to sharks the size of a sedan, there's no denying that the ocean is a particularly dangerous place. What many swimmers fail to realize, however, is that the ocean itself can be far more deadly than any of the creatures that inhabit it. When faced with the option of a school of hammerheads or a rip current—a narrow band of water that flows away from land and toward the open ocean—you should go with the hammerheads every single time. But if you do get caught in a rip current, you should . . .

■ Save Your Strength

A rip current (also known as a rip tide) forms as a result of waves breaking close to shore, and can move at speeds greater than 5 mph— approximately ½ mile per hour faster than humans swim. This means that even a strong swimmer will struggle to overcome the current to make it back to shore. If you attempt to swim against the current, you will eventually tire and risk drowning. Instead of swimming straight to shore and wearing yourself out, your first thoughts should be to remain calm and plan your next move.

■ Plant Your Feet and Walk to Safety

Provided the water is shallow enough, you might be able to stand up while still keeping your head above water. Assuming the current is not strong enough to knock you off your feet, you should be able to slowly walk your way back to shore.

If you can't confidently walk back to shore because the current is too strong, or the water is simply too deep to stand, you will need to get the attention of a lifeguard by waving your arms and calling for help. Even if you consider yourself a strong swimmer, there's no reason to put your life at unnecessary risk out of pride.

■ Swim Out of the Current

If there is no lifeguard on duty, your only hope is to get yourself out of the current. Luckily, rip currents tend to be relatively narrow, so you should be able to extricate yourself from the situation by swimming parallel to the shoreline. Be aware that the current will pull you away from shore as you swim; this is nothing to be concerned about. Most rip currents taper off less than 100 yards from shore, at which point you should stop drifting. Just keep your mind focused on swimming the short distance you will need to travel to reach the current's edge. If you get tired, rest by floating on your back until you are ready to continue.

Once you are safely free of the current, begin to make your way back to shore. While you may be desperate to reach dry land at this point, take it slow so you don't overexert yourself. The last thing you want is to make it this far, only to drown just a few feet from salvation.

I'm Trapped in an Avalanche

- **Likelihood of Happening:** Low
- **Ease of Prevention:** Low
- **Is Time a Factor?** Yes

There are a number of risks associated with winter hiking and skiing, ranging from broken bones and severe head injuries to frostbite and hypothermia. But one danger at the back of every winter adventure-seeker's mind is the threat of an avalanche. Although rare, a moving wall of snow can materialize in seconds and can leave you dazed, disoriented, and trapped.

■ Avoid the Avalanche and Hold on Tight

Chances are you will have little time to react once you realize there's a sheet of ice and snow hurtling toward you. But in the few moments you do have, try your best to move perpendicular to the path of the avalanche. If you are carrying any heavy, nonessential gear like skis or a backpack full of clothes, drop them immediately to help you move faster. You may just avoid the avalanche altogether if you can make it to the outskirts before it reaches you.

If you don't have time to move very far, make your way to a large tree or other sturdy object and attempt to hold on as the avalanche rushes past you. The longer you can hold on, the more likely you are to avoid being buried too deeply. However, if you are swept away, you can rise to the surface of the avalanche by swiftly kicking your feet and moving your arms as if you were swimming. Increase the chance that you will have access to fresh oxygen by lying on your back as you do so. This ensures that you will come to a stop facing toward the surface.

■ Know Which Way Is Up

Once both you and the snow have stopped moving, you will likely be completely disoriented and confused. Before you start worrying about escaping, your first task is to dig a small air pocket near your nose and mouth to ensure you are able to breathe. Snow can harden quickly after an avalanche, so it is important that you do this immediately.

Next, try to establish which direction is up by spitting onto the snow and observing which way the liquid travels. Gravity will cause it to fall toward the earth, so you can be certain the opposite direction is up. If you are close to the surface, you may be able to dig your way out before the snow hardens.

■ Call for Help

If you were not traveling with a locator beacon when the avalanche occurred, it will be difficult or impossible for rescuers to find you. With that in mind, your best hope for survival will be to call out for help when you hear people nearby. Because you have a limited air supply, only call for help in short, calculated bursts. If nobody is responding, conserve your air and energy for another attempt later. It may take rescuers some time to locate you, but try to remain calm and remind yourself that help is on its way.

I'm Trapped on a Chairlift

- **Likelihood of Happening:** Low
- **Ease of Prevention:** Low
- **Is Time a Factor?** Yes

Being temporarily stuck on a chairlift is rarely cause for alarm. In fact, it's not uncommon to find yourself suspended several dozen feet above the ground for a minute or two while the lift slows to allow a group of skiers more time to situate themselves on the chair, or simply because the lift is experiencing technical difficulties. But what if it's a matter of hours, or even days, instead of minutes?

■ You're Already Dressed for the Occasion

Unlike many survival situations, you couldn't be better outfitted to withstand the cold than you are while skiing. Your insulated jacket, boots, and gloves could keep you warm indefinitely, as long as the temperature doesn't sink below the survivability rating of your gear. With that in mind, as long as it's still light out, your best move is to sit tight and hope help arrives shortly. If you have a cell phone or walkie-talkie on hand, you should be able to alert someone on the ground to your situation.

When in Doubt, Burn Your Cash

In 2010, German snowboarder Dominik Podolsky found himself stranded on a chairlift for six hours after an Austrian ski resort closed for the night. He was finally rescued when a snow groomer noticed smoke coming from the chair. Podolsky had been burning the contents of his wallet, and was down to his last €20 note when he was spotted.

■ Survive Through the Night

As the sun sets and the temperature drops, you may be trapped on the lift for the night. To keep warm during the night, you can huddle together with your fellow survivors or place chemical hand warmers inside your jacket to keep your core temperature from dropping. If you are alone on the lift, try a light activity involving your upper body, like shadow boxing. Just make sure to avoid sweating, as this can actually increase your risk of hypothermia.

■ Jump for It

In dire circumstances, you may have no choice but to jump. And while you risk injuring yourself and making your situation worse by doing this, there are some steps you can take to reduce that risk.

First, remove your skis, as leaving them on could result in considerable injury if you land at an awkward angle. Next, make sure the bar of the chair is raised and you are completely unobstructed. Slowly inch yourself off the lift so that your lower torso is dangling off the edge, while you cling to the lift with your upper body. The farther down you can lower yourself in this manner the better, as this will reduce the height of your fall.

As you dangle, try to aim for the area beneath you where you feel the snow is deepest. Before you let yourself go, focus on bending your knees slightly before impact, as this will absorb some of the shock of hitting the ground. Finally, just after impact, try to roll yourself forward to further cushion the blow. With a little luck, you've managed to make it through your descent without serious injury and can head back to safety.

I Fall Through Ice

- **Likelihood of Happening:** Low
- **Ease of Prevention:** Moderate
- **Is Time a Factor?** Yes

Winter activities like ice-skating or snowmobiling can be fun, but there's an inherent risk that goes along with them. If the weather is warm, or you misjudge the thickness of the ice, your lighthearted outing could become a life or death struggle in the blink of an eye if you fall through.

■ Reorient Yourself and Get Moving

If you are "lucky," you've only been submerged for a moment and have popped back up in the same hole you fell through. If you weren't so lucky, you will need to first find the location of the hole and then swim towards it.

Once you've broken the surface of the water, act fast. The cold will quickly suck the dexterity from your hands and fingers, which will make escape increasingly difficult. To calm yourself, focus your immediate efforts on breathing steadily and keeping your head above water. Next, move yourself toward the area of ice where you were just before you fell through. The ice at other edges of the hole may be weak, but you can be fairly confident that the ice is strongest where you were recently on top of it. If you can't make it there, then head to whichever edge is closest that appears sturdy.

■ Hoist Yourself to Freedom

You will most likely need to pull yourself out of the water on your own. Place your arms firmly on the shelf of ice, and start to slowly pull your upper body up and out of the water. Don't worry if it takes a while or you are having trouble; just keep reminding yourself that you *do* have the strength to do it.

After you get your upper torso mostly out of the water and onto the ice, lean your weight forward and kick your feet as hard as you can while you attempt to pull yourself up and out with your arms. If you don't make it on the first attempt, keep trying.

Once you are completely out of the water and on the ice, do not attempt to stand up. At present your weight is evenly distributed along the ice, and you want to keep it that way. Slowly roll yourself away from the hole until you feel confident that you can stand safely.

How a Screwdriver Can Save Your Life

When walking in areas where you know there is a risk of falling through ice, it's wise to carry a set of safety spikes (small pointed sticks that you can use to grip the ice and pull yourself out). While you can buy a dedicated set, a Phillips-head screwdriver with a loop of paracord or string several inches long can work just as well.

■ Warm Yourself Up

Once you're out of the water, you are still in very serious danger of becoming hypothermic. If you are close to civilization, head straight for the nearest home or car to warm yourself up. Remove all of your wet clothes and wrap yourself in blankets. If possible, run a lukewarm bath and submerge yourself, raising the water temperature slightly as you warm up. If you can't find shelter, start a fire immediately and stay close to it until you are comfortable enough to head for safety.

I Drive Into Water

Likelihood of Happening: Low
Ease of Prevention: Moderate
Is Time a Factor? Yes

Almost nobody intends to veer their car into an open body of water, but it happens. Weather conditions could obstruct your view, causing you to miss a curve in the road. An animal could step out into the road and force you to swerve. But at this point, how you came to be trapped in a sinking car is irrelevant—what's important is getting out of it.

■ Use SCWO

Just like elementary school math, surviving an escape from a sinking automobile has an order of operations, called SCWO:

- **Seat belt:** As soon as your car stops moving, release your seat belt. If you save this step for last, you could find yourself trapped.
- **Children:** Assist any children with the removal of their own seatbelts.
- **Window:** While the car's electric system is still functioning, lower the driver-side window. If you are unable to roll down the window,

you will need to break it with an object you have on hand, like a shoe or a devoted safety hammer.

- **Out:** Help any children escape through the window and then exit yourself. Swim away from the car and head for shore.

Keep in mind that the average automobile will float for anywhere from thirty seconds to several minutes. If you keep calm and remember the SCWO steps, you should be able to evacuate the car safely before it sinks.

■ Be Prepared to Escape from the Bottom

If you were unable to lower the window quickly enough and can't break through it, then your only option is to sit calmly until the pressure in the car equals that of the water outside. Translation: your car is going to fill up with water with you inside. As this happens, keep calm and instruct any children present to follow your lead. Breathe normally until the water level reaches your chest. Once it does, take a big gulp of air, open the door, ensure any children in the car are able to make it out, and begin swimming toward the surface. If you find you are disoriented, expel a small bubble of air and follow the direction it travels.

I See Someone Drowning

- **Likelihood of Happening:** Moderate
- **Ease of Prevention:** Low
- **Is Time a Factor?** Yes

Nobody wants to be in a situation where someone else's life depends on them, but sometimes, in our ordinary lives, we find ourselves in extraordinary circumstances. Whether you are taking a casual stroll by a river or are enjoying a quiet canoe ride on a lake, if you spot someone who needs assistance you may only have a few precious moments to save her life.

■ Think First, but Act Fast

Before you go jumping into the water, you'll want to consider a few variables. First, is the suspected drowning victim actually in danger? Call out to the individual to see if she is capable of communicating her need for help. If she can't respond and is thrashing about with her head just above the water, it's likely she needs assistance.

Next, you will need to determine if it is safe to enter the water. If the water is especially choppy, the victim appears to be caught in a rip current, or entering the water would require a long freefall, your only option may be to call for help. It's also important to be mindful of your own abilities as a swimmer. If you are not confident that you can aid the victim without putting yourself in danger, you should not enter the water.

■ Approach the Victim with Caution

Once you are in the water, be very careful as you move closer to the victim. In an act of desperation, she may grab onto you and pull you down under the water. With that in mind, the safest way to approach the victim is from behind.

Wedge your forearms under the victim's armpits and raise her head above the water so she can take a breath. Once the victim has relaxed, you can slowly start swimming back to shore. Take short, gentle strokes and keep encouraging the victim as you go, reminding her that everything is going to be all right.

■ Get Professional Help

Once ashore, immediately dial 911 or instruct a bystander to do so. Even if the victim shows no outward signs of trauma, she may not realize that she is seriously injured due to the adrenaline running through her system.

If the victim is unresponsive and you are the only person present, place your ear next to her mouth and feel for breath on the side of your face. You can also look at her chest to see if her lungs are expanding and deflating. If there are no signs of breathing, check for a pulse for a period of ten seconds. If there is none, tilt the victim's head back, lift her chin slightly, pinch her nose closed, cover her mouth with your own, and give two short breaths. Next, place the heel of one hand at the center of the victim's chest and perform thirty chest compressions to the beat of "Stayin' Alive" by the Bee Gees. Repeat the cycle of breaths and compression until breathing resumes or help arrives.

I Get Lost on a Day Hike

Likelihood of Happening: Low
Ease of Prevention: High
Is Time a Factor? Yes

Nobody sets out on a scenic trek in the woods expecting to get lost. Yet every year thousands of hikers find themselves disoriented, with the sun quickly setting on the horizon. Whether it's a simple matter of poor time management or you are well and truly lost, your ability to plan ahead and remain calm increase your chances of survival exponentially.

■ STOP

When many hikers realize they are lost, they immediately slip into panic mode and start frantically searching for the trail—which causes them to get even more lost. Instead, you should adhere to the STOP acronym.

- **Stop:** The moment you start to suspect you might be lost, immediately stop moving. Take off your pack and sit down on a rock or log. Take a few sips of water and calm down.
- **Think:** What was the last identifiable landmark you remember passing? Can you backtrack to that point and use it to find your way back? Take out your map and try to remember where you might have left the trail.
- **Observe:** Can you hear or see a road, trail, river, or any large topographical feature that might help you find your location on the map? Are there any trail blazes in the area that you might have missed?
- **Plan:** Take stock of your supplies and formulate a plan. Do you have the gear necessary to survive a night out in the elements? Can you confidently hike yourself back to a trail before sunset?

The Universal Language of Distress

If you happen to have a whistle with you, three evenly spaced toots is the universally understood signal for help. The same is true for those lost hunting, who can fire three shots in succession, pausing after each shot.

■ Stay Put and Wait for Help to Arrive

Before starting on any hike, it's imperative that you alert a friend or family member where you will be going and when you plan to return. If you've taken this step, then help will soon be on the way. Your main goal now is to sit tight and stay warm. Hopefully you have extra clothes and materials for an emergency shelter, but if you've neglected to bring them, your best bet is to seek shelter in an area that's out of the wind— like behind a large rock or tree.

Building a fire will also go a long way toward staving off hypothermia and keeping your spirits up. In addition to this, assuming there's no cell phone service and your walkie-talkies are broken (or forgotten), your fire can also act as a signal for rescuers to alert them of your location. To increase the likelihood that the smoke from your fire will be seen, choose a wide clearing on high ground if possible and build a second signal fire. Once your fire is burning steadily, you can place green vegetation on top to create more smoke. You can also lie out your pack or any brightly colored clothing to attract the attention of anyone searching from the air.

Even if you are absolutely 100 percent confident you can walk yourself out, staying in one location is still your best chance of making it home safely.

I'm Being Robbed at Gunpoint

- **Likelihood of Happening:** Low
- **Ease of Prevention:** Low
- **Is Time a Factor?** No

Unfortunately, more than 100,000 people are robbed at gunpoint every year in the United States. While the majority make it out of the situation unharmed, failing to react appropriately could put you in serious danger.

▓ Lose Your Wallet, not Your Life

"Lose your wallet, not your life" is a tired saying, but an accurate one. The first advice any law enforcement agent will give you about dealing with an armed assailant is to comply with their demands. While it may be frustrating to part with your personal belongings, you can replace your credit cards, cash, and phone with relative ease.

Be slow and deliberate with your movements as you reach for your personal items to hand them over. In a calm, collected voice, narrate your actions while you interact with the assailant. For example, clearly state, "I'm reaching for my wallet now." If you move too quickly, or reach for an unknown object without disclosing that to your assailant, he may panic and discharge his firearm, either accidentally or from fear that you were reaching for a weapon.

▓ Observe and Retain

While it can be difficult to maintain your composure in a life-threatening situation, your ability to scrutinize your assailant and memorize his face greatly increases the chances that police will be able to detain him later and prevent future attacks. Pay close attention to general details like his height, weight, estimated age, and clothes, as well as more specific things like unusual scars or tattoos that might help identify him.

When the mugger leaves, take note of the direction in which he flees and memorize the license plate number if he escapes in a car. If you still have your phone, proceed to a safe, public location and dial 911. An officer will arrive to take your statement and begin the process of tracking down the individual responsible. Under no circumstances should you give chase or attempt to apprehend the assailant.

I'm Choking

- **Likelihood of Happening:** High
- **Ease of Prevention:** Moderate
- **Is Time a Factor?** Yes

As a species, humans may sit comfortably at the top of the food chain, but during our evolution we developed one unfortunate vulnerability. The location of the larynx, which provides humans with the gift of speech, also prevents us from breathing and eating simultaneously. This is not much of a big deal as far as handicaps go—unless, of course, something happens to get stuck down there.

■ Enlist the Help of Others

If you are able to cough, then the obstruction is only partially blocking your airway and you might be able to dislodge the offending food item simply by coughing it up. If you are unable to clear the obstruction quickly by coughing, however, someone will need to intervene on your behalf. Unfortunately, one side effect of choking is it makes it difficult or even impossible to speak. So you will need another way to communicate to your fellow diners that you need assistance.

While most people will realize there's a problem when they notice you gasping for air, you should employ the universal nonverbal signal for choking by clutching both hands to your throat. Once someone in your party realizes the gravity of the situation, she should immediately call 911. Your best hope for clearing the airway is that someone nearby is trained to perform the Heimlich maneuver. If not, a series of blows to the back could be enough to eliminate the obstruction.

■ Perform the Heimlich Maneuver on Yourself

There are few things more terrifying than the prospect of choking alone at home. While it may be difficult, your first goal will be to calm down so you can think clearly and quickly. Then you will want to try to cough up the object, if there is a partial obstruction. If you are unable to cough, you'll need to find a stable piece of furniture at waist height to use to perform a self-Heimlich maneuver.

To do this, first make your dominant hand into a tight fist and place it against your abdomen, just above your belly button. Then place your other hand flat on top of your first. Next, lean your body onto the chair, desk, table, or other stationary object so that your arms rest between the object and your body. Once you are in position, drive your fist up into your abdomen in one quick motion while pressing your body toward the solid object. If the obstruction remains, continue thrusting until you force it out of your airway.

I'm Caught in a Lightning Storm

— **Likelihood of Happening:** High
— **Ease of Prevention:** Low
— **Is Time a Factor?** No

Every second, approximately 100 bolts of lightning strike somewhere on the planet. Each strike contains more than 5 billion joules of power and can reach temperatures higher than 90,000°F. While the vast majority of those strikes are of little danger to people, that's small consolation when you are stuck in an open field watching the sky light up like a Christmas tree.

■ Seek Shelter—but Make Sure It's a Good One

When it comes to lightning, you need a little more than four walls and a roof to ensure your safety. While a tool shed, tent, or even a portable toilet will shield you from the rain, the structure must contain some means to ground the lightning, such as plumbing or wiring, to be safe in a thunderstorm.

If you can safely do so, make your way to a large, well-constructed building. Once inside, stay away from any landline phones and avoid washing your hands or taking a shower. You will also want to avoid touching any metal surfaces that extend to the exterior of the building, such as door handles, window frames, or any exposed wires.

A car will also make a suitable shelter, provided the windows are closed and you keep your body clear of any metal surfaces in the vehicle's interior.

■ Get Low and Stay Low

While the idea that lightning will only strike the tallest available object is a myth, it is true that tall structures like billboards, trees, and telephone poles are more likely to be the site of a lightning strike than short ones. With that in mind, you will want to distance yourself from any tall structures (unless you're inside them), while also making sure that you're not in an open field.

Find a low ditch or ravine approximately 100 feet from any tall structures or metallic objects and crouch down, with your feet firmly planted on the ground and your head tucked between your legs. Should you be struck, this posture will hopefully allow the lightning to pass over your body without damaging your internal organs.

■ Wait until It's Safe

Many lightning strikes occur because the victim believes the storm has passed and leaves shelter prematurely. Most experts recommend waiting at least thirty minutes after the last sounds of thunder vanish out of earshot before resuming outdoor activities. If you believe there may still be storms in the area, remain indoors until you are certain it is safe to venture outside. As you move around outside, be careful of any exposed electrical wires that may have been knocked down by high winds or falling trees.

A Car Hits Me While I'm Walking

— **Likelihood of Happening:** Moderate
— **Ease of Prevention:** Moderate
— **Is Time a Factor?** No

We live in a world where different forms of transportation are designed to coexist in relative harmony. Bicycles travel on the same roads as cars and motorcycles, and crosswalks allow humans to safely move from one coffee shop to another. Unfortunately, this delicate system doesn't always play out as it should, and accidents do happen.

■ Anticipate the Accident

As a pedestrian, you have a much wider field of vision than someone driving a car, and it's possible you will have a small amount of time to react to the impending impact. While it may just be an instant, this could be more than enough time to save your life.

Your head is the most vulnerable part of your body in the event of a collision, and you will want to use your arms and hands to protect it before, during, and after the impact. If there's time, grasp your hands together at the back of your head and tuck your head down toward your chest.

After you're struck, try your best to maneuver your body so your back is toward the car's windshield. Most modern cars are equipped with safety glass, which will help cushion the blow. While it may be difficult, try to roll your way up and over the roof of the car to avoid being propelled ahead of the car then underneath its tires.

■ Get Help and Keep Movements to a Minimum

You've just been struck by several thousand pounds of metal and plastic traveling at a considerable speed, so you've likely sustained at least a few minor injuries, and maybe a major injury, as well. Although you may not be immediately aware of something serious due to the adrenaline and other hormones coursing through your system, the safest option is to assume the worst. It's possible you may have sustained serious neck or back injuries, which could be exacerbated should you attempt to move. With that in mind, do not attempt to stand up and walk around. You should only move if your position in the road puts you at risk for being run over by another passing car.

Hopefully the driver will remain on the scene to call 911, or, at the very least, someone who witnessed the accident will step in to lend a hand. Assuming there is nobody around, use your cell phone to get help if it is undamaged, or call out to people passing by who might not be able to see you in your current position.

■ Exchange Information

Assuming your injuries do not prevent you from communicating with the driver, you should get his or her name, phone number, and insurance information as you wait for the ambulance to arrive. This will allow you to file a police report, as well as open a claim with the driver's insurance company to cover the cost of any medical expenses. If possible, also take down the name and number of anyone nearby who may have witnessed the accident.

I've Been Shot

— **Likelihood of Happening:** Low
— **Ease of Prevention:** Low
— **Is Time a Factor?** Yes

Regardless of your opinions about gun ownership, there's no denying that guns are dangerous. This can be a good thing if you are using one to defend yourself or your home, but if you are on the receiving end of an intentional or accidental gunshot—like approximately 100,000 Americans a year are—then you will learn firsthand just how effective guns can be at causing debilitating damage.

■ Get Out of Harm's Way

Assuming whoever shot you did so on purpose, you don't want to give the assailant the opportunity to finish the job. Depending on how well you are able to move, you will either want to run to a safe location or barricade yourself inside a locked room. If you don't have any other options, hide underneath furniture, behind parked cars, inside closets, or anywhere that provides some level of concealment.

If you are unable to move and the gunman is approaching, you may be able to trick him into believing you are dead. Keep your breathing as shallow as possible and do your best to remain as still as possible until the gunman has moved on.

If you were struck as the result of a hunting accident or the wound was inadvertently self-inflicted, make sure that any guns are secured and pointed away from anyone in the vicinity before you address your wounds.

■ Provide Preliminary Medical Care

Whether the bullet merely grazed your shoulder or you were shot in the stomach at point-blank range, you will need immediate medical attention. If it is safe to use your cell phone, immediately call 911 and alert the operator to your location. If you are unable to call for help, or there is an active shooting situation that will prevent emergency services from arriving, you will need to provide preliminary care yourself.

How you treat the wound as you wait for help to arrive will depend on where you were shot.

- **Arms and Legs:** To help control bleeding, lie down and elevate the site of the wound above the heart. Only apply a tourniquet if the bleeding is so severe that failing to do so could result in death.
- **Head:** Lie down and keep the head slightly elevated by placing a towel, clothes, or other object underneath.
- **Neck:** Apply pressure, but be careful that you do not restrict blood flow from the carotid arteries to the brain or obstruct your breathing.

- **Chest and Back:** Do not elevate the legs, as this will only increase the flow of blood from the wound. Seal the wound with plastic wrap to prevent air from traveling in and out as you breathe.

Regardless of what body part was shot, it is also important to be aware of the possible presence of an exit wound. If possible, pressure should be applied to both the entrance and exit wounds until help arrives.

Give Yourself a Hand

While there isn't a good location to take a bullet, your odds of survival are highest if you are struck in the hands. They don't contain any major arteries, and the bullet will likely pass through without releasing all of its kinetic energy.

I've Been Bitten by a Snake

Likelihood of Happening: Low
Ease of Prevention: Moderate
Is Time a Factor? Yes

The philosophy that an animal is more afraid of you than you are of it is especially true when it comes to snakes. Most species will tuck tail and run the moment they sense you coming anywhere near them. But when fleeing isn't an option, or the snake feels threatened by your presence, the majority of snakes will rely on the only defense they have: a lightning-fast bite with their dagger-like fangs. While it's true that not all snakes possess fangs, it's best to assume you are dealing with a species that does.

■ Observe the Snake

Of all the known species of snakes, only about 15 percent are venomous. So the odds are heavily in your favor that you have nothing to worry about beyond a little blood and painful puncture wounds. If the snake is still in the vicinity, observe it from a safe distance to help determine if it was indeed venomous. Some signs to look out for include:

- **Triangular Heads:** If a snake is venomous, the venom glands (located at the base of the head) generally cause the head to take on a triangular appearance.
- **Bright Colors:** Vibrant yellows, reds, greens, and other hues are often attributed to venomous snakes. Be careful, however, as many harmless snakes mimic the patterns of venomous species to deter predators.
- **Rattles:** Several species of venomous rattlesnake can be identified by the unique, ribbed appendage at the tip of their tail that produces their telltale sound.
- **Slit Pupils:** While not true of all venomous snakes, many species possess thin, vertical pupils as opposed to rounded ones.

While many venomous snakes possess similar traits, it's better to assume the worst than to ignore a potentially lethal bite because you misidentified the snake you encountered as harmless.

■ Get Help Fast

Assuming the snake was venomous, your ultimate goal is to get yourself to a hospital as quickly as possible to receive antivenom and other medical treatment. If you are at home, call for an ambulance or have a friend or relative drive you. Do not attempt to drive yourself, as there is a significant risk that you could lose consciousness en route. As you travel, do your best to remain calm and keep your heart rate down. If you become anxious, your rapid heartbeat will pump the venom through your body at an accelerated rate.

If you are hiking in the wilderness, waiting for an ambulance or even a helicopter to come and rescue you simply may not be an option. There's a good chance you will have to walk yourself to a highway in order to get the medical care you need.

Before you get moving, take a moment to apply a constriction band an inch above the location of the bite. Unlike a tourniquet, which can limit blood flow to the area to dangerous levels, a constriction band will slow the spread of the venom while still allowing some blood flow. If you do not have a constriction band on hand, you can tie a bandana or piece of cloth loosely enough so that you can fit one finger between it and the skin.

If you have a backpack, take only your water and leave the bag and any of its contents behind. The less weight you have to carry, the less you will need to exert yourself. As you walk, make sure to take long, even breaths, and slow down if you notice your heart rate increasing. As long as you remain calm, you should be able to make it out in time to get the medical attention you need.

The Power Goes Out in Winter

- **Likelihood of Happening:** High
- **Ease of Prevention:** Low
- **Is Time a Factor?** Yes

Losing power is merely an excuse to break out the board games and wait patiently for it to come back on, right? Unfortunately, losing power can mean more than a fun night with your family—especially if it happens during a winter storm.

In December of 2013, a massive ice storm hit the Midwest and Northeastern United States, dumping a substantial amount of ice and snow throughout the country. The added stress felled countless trees and left millions of residents without power for upwards of two weeks, resulting in twenty-seven deaths.

While this isn't the norm, it's fairly easy to prepare yourself and your home to weather a similar catastrophe.

■ React Immediately

As soon as your power goes out, you need to spring into action. The first thing you should do is locate your flashlights and herd your family into one central location, preferably a small room that you can close off from the rest of the house. This will allow you to conserve heat. If you have a fireplace, use that as your primary heat source, but use your dry wood sparingly if you don't have a substantial supply. If you don't have a fireplace, rely on warm clothing and blankets to keep warm.

The contents of your refrigerator will quickly spoil, so eat the most perishable items first and move the rest into a cooler with ice. Avoid leaving food outside, as temperature variations can make food unsafe to eat, but use any accumulated snow to replace the ice in your cooler.

Without the benefit of a heating system, the drop in temperature could quickly cause your pipes to freeze. To prevent this, run a slow trickle of water from your faucets. If you haven't already stocked up on water, now is also a good time to fill up any empty containers, as well as your bathtub.

■ Hunker Down

If you don't have the luxury of traveling to a location that still has power, you will need to make do with what you have. Staying hydrated, well nourished, and warm should be your main concerns until the power comes back on. You may need to start rationing your food and water as time goes on, but at first you should use as much as you need to stay comfortable.

To keep warm, dress yourself in layers and pay close attention to your head and hands. Wear a wool hat that covers your ears, and mittens or gloves. This is especially important when you are sleeping, as your body temperature drops. Keep trips outside to a minimum, to avoid opening and closing exterior doors. Block any drafts around windows and doors using towels and blankets, and be sure to close any blinds and curtains to trap in heat.

Whether it's a matter of hours, days, or weeks, rest assured that the power will come back on eventually, and your life will get back to normal.

My Tire Blows Out

— **Likelihood of Happening:** Moderate
— **Ease of Prevention:** High
— **Is Time a Factor?** No

When you first learned how to drive, you probably spent a lot of time avoiding disasters. Maybe you constantly checked your blind spot before merging, always used your turn signals, and were cautious to stay a safe distance behind the car in front of you. But for things that are out of your control, like a tire blowout on the highway, you may still be dangerously ill prepared.

■ Ignore Your Instincts

When most people hear the loud pop of a tire blowing out, they usually slam on the brakes and try to pull over to the shoulder. Unfortunately, this is also the worst thing you can do at 65 mph.

Following a sudden loss of tire pressure, the vehicle will inevitably veer to whichever side the blowout occurred on. As a result, the driver often overcompensates in an attempt to pull over by forcing the car in the opposite direction, or veers too hard in the same direction. Ultimately, this causes an accident.

Instead, in order to continue in a straight line, you want to keep your foot on the accelerator and steer in the opposite direction from which the car is veering.

■ Slow Down

Now that you have gained some semblance of control over your vehicle, it's time to gradually come to a halt. While you shouldn't slam on the brakes, you should slowly take your foot off the accelerator and allow the car to slow down on its own. The drag from the flat tire will slow the vehicle rather quickly, even without assistance from your brakes. Once you have reduced your speed to a safer and more manageable 30 mph, you can very gently begin to apply the brake and pull over.

■ Stay Put and Buckle Up

While it is generally safe to get out and change a tire on a rustic country road, doing the same on a busy highway isn't a great idea. If you exit your vehicle on the interstate, you could easily be struck by a passing motorist, or cause another accident should a vehicle swerve to miss you. Instead, remain buckled in your seat and use a cell phone to contact the police or call for a tow service. If you don't have a cell phone, hang a white object out of the window to indicate that you need assistance.

My Car Breaks Down in Winter

- **Likelihood of Happening:** Moderate
- **Ease of Prevention:** Moderate
- **Is Time a Factor?** Yes

Having your car break down in the warmer months is certainly a pain, but a disabled vehicle can be a death sentence when the outside temperature drops. In an ideal situation, you will be able to phone for help or flag down a passing motorist. But if your cell phone is dead or was damaged in an accident, or if there's no service in the area, you may need to hunker down until help arrives.

■ Settle In

In the best-case scenario, your car has merely broken down on the side of the road and a passing motorist will send help within a few hours. In this situation, you will just need to remain in the car and keep warm.

In the worst-case scenario, you've driven your car off the road into a ditch. This is especially problematic, as you won't be visible from the road, and damage to your car may allow cold air to enter. If the damage is severe, you might even be trapped and unable to exit the vehicle. If this is the case, while circumstances are bleak, there are steps you can take to improve your situation.

The first step is to access your survival kit—which should include items like road flares, a first-aid kit, a flashlight, an emergency blanket, warm clothes, nonperishable food, water, and a small camping stove with extra fuel—and don your warm clothes. If your car is still operational, turn the heater on for ten minutes every hour to stay warm. You will need to crack the windows slightly to avoid carbon monoxide poisoning, in case the exhaust pipe is obstructed. Next, turn on an inside light to make your car as visible as possible.

> **Surviving in a Death Trap**
>
> In 2012, Peter Skyllberg, a 44-year-old Swedish man, was pulled from a disabled car in the woods a mile away from a deserted road near the town of Umea. He had survived for nearly two months, sustaining himself on nothing but a small amount of food he had in his car and handfuls of snow. During his ordeal, temperatures plunged to −22°F.

■ Stay Put and Stay Hydrated

If you've prepared ahead of time, you should have enough food and water to last you a few days. While you can go weeks without food, you have a few days at best without drinking, so don't hesitate to drink plenty of water. If you run out, you can melt snow with your car's heater or use the portable camping stove in your survival kit—just be sure to crack a window or exit the vehicle first to allow gases to escape.

If help does not arrive quickly, it can be tempting to exit the vehicle and attempt to walk to safety. While this may be necessary if you run out of supplies, it is far safer to remain in your vehicle for as long as possible. Exposure to the elements can be life threatening in just a matter of hours.

I Wake Up to a Fire

- **Likelihood of Happening:** Low
- **Ease of Prevention:** Moderate
- **Is Time a Factor?** Yes

You hopefully have a smoke alarm in every room, but despite our near-universal diligence when it comes to alerting ourselves of the presence of fire, few people have planned out what to do with that information beyond "flee in terror, quickly."

■ React Immediately

While every home is different, the typical house fire will double in size every one to two minutes. So time is of the essence. The moment you hear your fire alarm go off is not a cue to debate whether the land-lord is conducting a test he neglected to warn you about. It's a cue to act. Don't stop to grab your phone. Don't start searching for your wedding album. Just get up and start moving.

At this point you know there's smoke, and that somewhere in your home is fire. But you don't know where. And hopefully you won't find out until you are safely outside. But before you make it out, you have to first leave your bedroom.

If you are on the first floor, or your building is outfitted with fire escapes, exiting through the window may be your safest option. Barring that, you'll want to use the back of your hand to check the bedroom door and knob for heat. Even if the door is cool, you should still proceed with caution and brace your shoulder against the door as you open it to prevent a sudden backdraft from knocking you to the ground. If heat and smoke enter, the fire could be on the other side and you will need to use another exit.

■ Stay Low and Keep Moving

Running toward the exit might seem like the best option, but in a smoke-filled room the safest approach is to crouch down or crawl. This puts as much distance as possible between you and the smoke, which rises to the ceiling. Smoke inhalation can render you unconscious in a matter of minutes, so it is important to limit your exposure to it as much as possible. If you can, use a wet towel to cover your mouth to prevent the smoke from entering your lungs. If you don't have time for that, use your hands instead. If you share an apartment with friends or family, yell to them as you move toward the exit to alert them of the fire.

■ Stay Calm

If the bedroom door is hot and you can't safely exit through the window, the most important thing you can do is to remain calm and remind yourself that help is coming. Until it does arrive, you can improve your situation by sealing the cracks in the door with bedding to prevent the smoke from entering your room.

Smoke Alarms Are Never Foolproof

While smoke alarms are the single most important fire safety tool at your disposal, it's important to remember they are by no means foolproof. According to the National Fire Prevention Association, battery-powered smoke detectors fail in 21 percent of fires considered large enough to activate them. While significantly more efficient, hardwired alarms still have a failure rate of around 7 percent.

To alert those outside to your location, hang a bed sheet out the window or an article of white clothing. Just be sure to close the window again, as the fire could be drawn to the oxygen pouring in if you don't.

There's an Earthquake

- **Likelihood of Happening:** Low
- **Ease of Prevention:** Low
- **Is Time a Factor?** Yes

Earthquakes are one of the most common natural disasters and can occur anywhere on the planet. While the vast majority are so minor that they may go entirely unnoticed, major earthquakes can cause billions of dollars in damage and put hundreds of thousands of lives at risk.

■ Treat Every Tremor Like It's the Big One

Early warning systems to predict earthquakes have improved with advances in technology, but they still only offer several seconds to a few minutes of advance warning. This means that the first indication most earthquake victims receive will be the initial tremors caused by the earthquake.

Earthquakes are rated on a scale of 0 to 10 based on the energy released by the event, a measurement system known as the Richter scale. While serious damage does not usually occur as a result of earthquakes below 7.0, it is relatively common for large earthquakes to be preceded by smaller foreshocks. For this reason, it is always safest to take immediate precautions, even during relatively small tremors.

Tweets Travel Faster Than Shockwaves

When a magnitude 5.8 earthquake hit Virginia in the summer of 2011, residents immediately posted news of the event to social media sites like Twitter. Even though it took the shockwaves—traveling approximately five miles per second—less than a minute to reach New York City, Manhattanites were able to read about the impending quake before they even felt the first tremors.

■ Take Cover

If you're indoors, the philosophy that you should stand in a doorway to protect yourself during an earthquake sounds logical, but the truth is that most doorframes are no more sturdy than the rest of the building. What's worse, standing in one offers the additional risk of being injured by the door should it swing about violently. Instead, most experts now recommend you drop to the ground and crouch beneath a sturdy piece of furniture like a table or desk, and hold on to it tightly. Ideally, head for something that is a safe distance from any windows, glass fixtures, or heavy furniture like bookshelves that could come crashing down. You have a very limited amount of time to seek shelter, so if the room in which you are currently standing does not offer any reasonable cover, simply duck down on the ground and use your arms to protect your head. If you attempt to run to another room, you could fall and be seriously injured by unsecured objects in your home.

If you're outdoors when an earthquake strikes, first move away from any large objects that might topple as a result of the earthquake. Old buildings, large trees, street lamps, telephone poles, and billboards could easily crush you under their weight, or leave you pinned and trapped. If you are driving, distance yourself from any large objects, stop the car, and turn off the engine. Leave your seat belt buckled, lean your upper torso down towards your legs, and cover your head with your arms. Do not attempt to leave your vehicle until the shaking has ceased.

■ Be Cautious

Even though it may appear safe to move around, you still may feel numerous aftershocks following an earthquake. Be mindful of the potential threat and be prepared to seek cover immediately should the earth begin to shake again.

While walking about your home, be careful of broken glass or other hazards that might impede your ability to move around. If you smell gas, immediately exit your home and call the gas company.

When moving around outdoors, pay special attention to any downed electrical wires. The earthquake may also have created large uneven patches in roads and walkways, so proceed with caution.

A Riot Erupts Around Me

Likelihood of Happening: Low
Ease of Prevention: Low
Is Time a Factor? No

Even if you live in a nice quiet town where nothing ever happens, mob mentality is nothing to take lightly. Something as small as a controversial defeat—or victory—in a local sporting event can be enough to turn a group of normally respectful individuals into a pack of dangerous animals. If you find yourself smack dab in the middle of a good old-fashioned riot, how you react could save your life.

■ Don't Be a Hero

You may firmly disagree with the agenda of the rioters, assuming they have one, but now is not the time to try to talk sense into anyone. You will have just as much luck appealing to an angry mob as you would a swarm of bees. Instead, keep your head down and calmly head for safety. You'll need to override your urge to run, as moving too quickly could attract the attention of the rioters. If you are with family or friends, remain in constant physical contact to avoid splitting up.

As you move, keep away from main roads and other areas where rioters are likely to congregate. For example, you'll be far safer traveling in residential neighborhoods than the business sector where there could be looting. Also avoid dead-end streets, tunnels, or any obstructions like fences and walls that could cause you to be cornered.

■ Get Indoors

Ultimately, your goal is to return to your home where you know you will be safe. If you are more than a few blocks away, however, you may need to find somewhere else to hunker down for a while. If possible, steer clear of any buildings containing valuable and desirable merchandise, like electronics stores or retail outlets. Also, while it may seem wise to go to the local pub to have a nice cold pint and wait for all of this to blow over, bars are a common target during riots and should be avoided.

Look for buildings with basements where you can hide and barricade the door if necessary. Local residents may be willing to shelter you until you can safely make your way back home, but keep in mind that they will also be on high alert. Don't be discouraged if everyone in the neighborhood refuses to answer their door. While you could simply break into an unoccupied home if you are in immediate danger, be aware of the additional risk of confrontation with the owner when he or she returns.

The World's Most Expensive Riot

In February 2002, fighting between Muslim and Hindu citizens in the Gujarat region of India erupted following an attack on an express train that killed fifty-eight people. The backlash lasted for months, left more than 1,000 people dead, and caused more than $1 billion in damage.

■ Batten Down the Hatches

Even if the riot appears to be dying down, don't assume that the danger has passed. The riot could easily start back up again, and you need to be prepared if it does.

First, lock all of the entrances to your home as well as any and all windows. If you feel you are at great risk for home invasion, consider barricading the windows either with boards or heavy furniture. Be careful to leave yourself at least two exits, as you will need to leave quickly in the case of a fire.

Next, move everyone in your home to the basement or a windowless room to avoid being injured by rocks, bricks, or other debris that could be thrown by rioters. Bring with you food, water, games to keep children distracted, and a radio to monitor the situation. Hopefully you will be able to move around freely soon, but you should be prepared to hunker down for as long as a few days.

CHAPTER 2

Loss of Limb, Serious Injuries, and Not-So-Serious Injuries

Nobody wakes up in the morning expecting to spill boiling-hot coffee on their lap or cut off their index finger with a table saw, but these sorts of things happen to thousands of people every day. While they may not be life threatening, that's small consolation when you realize you have to hike three miles down the side of a mountain with a broken ankle or pull a rusty nail out of your foot.

While it's true that many of life's unexpected bumps, bruises, cuts, and punctures will land you in the hospital, you'll be surprised what you can do with a little ingenuity and moderate knowledge of proper first aid.

I've Been Stabbed

Likelihood of Happening: Low
Ease of Prevention: Low
Is Time a Factor? Yes

Of the ways to be attacked, being stabbed is arguably the most terrifying. Guns are expensive, difficult to obtain, and produce a lot of noise when fired. On the other hand, knives are small, silent, easy to conceal, and can be purchased almost anywhere. Even more scary, in the hands of someone who wishes to do you harm, even everyday objects like glass bottles and pencils can become dangerous weapons.

■ Retreat to a Safe Location and Call for Help

Whether you've been stabbed at the climax of an argument or at random in a crowd, there's still a significant risk that whoever harmed you is still close by. If you are able to walk, immediately proceed to a well-lit public area or an enclosed building where you can lock or barricade yourself inside. Once you are safe, you can begin to address the wound.

Victims of stabbings often recall later that the experience felt more like being punched with a fist than punctured by a sharp object. As a result, you may not realize the severity of your wound(s) at first. Take a few moments to dial 911 and examine your entire body to check for any additional injuries.

■ Begin Treatment

Start by removing any clothes near the site of any stab wounds. This will make it easier to identify and treat the exact location of the wound.

If the object with which you were stabbed is still embedded in your body, leave it in place for now. Its presence could be minimizing blood loss, and removing it might put you at risk.

Find a clean towel or article of clothing and use it to apply firm pressure directly to the site of the wound, or closely around it, in the event that the knife or other object is still present. This should slow the bleeding considerably, but it may still be necessary to apply a tourniquet if profuse bleeding continues. Use a tourniquet only as a last resort when you feel you are at risk of bleeding to death otherwise. If your improvised bandage material becomes saturated with blood, simply add more material on top and continue to apply pressure. If you remove the saturated bandage, you will disrupt the clot and increase the bleeding. If there is tape available, or you are able to secure the bandage without inhibiting blood circulation, this will ensure that it remains in place.

Be mindful of the risk of shock as you wait for help. You can minimize this risk by covering yourself with a warm jacket or blankets and remaining as still and calm as possible.

I Think I've Been Drugged

— **Likelihood of Happening:** Low
— **Ease of Prevention:** Moderate
— **Is Time a Factor?** Yes

Alcohol is by far the most popular drug on earth. It's legal and readily available in the vast majority of countries, and is consumed by hundreds of millions of people every year. Unfortunately, its ubiquity provides the perfect opportunity for a malevolent individual to slip something a little stronger than whiskey into your glass.

Although designed to treat insomnia, the drug flunitrazepam—more commonly known as Rohypnol or "roofies"—is the drug of choice for sexual predators looking to incapacitate their intended victim. Most commonly, a pill is dissolved in a drink and then unknowingly ingested by the target.

■ Try to Get Help

The inherent mind-altering properties of alcohol can make it difficult for someone who has ingested flunitrazepam to realize they have been drugged. As the drug begins to take effect, you will likely believe you've had more to drink than you realized. If you do find yourself feeling uncharacteristically inebriated, immediately alert someone of the situation so they can get you to a hospital. The drug may cause you to lose consciousness, so it is important to have someone you trust who can help you.

If you are alone, immediately dial 911. Alert them of your location if you are able to communicate. Even if you can't talk, they still may be able to trace your call.

■ Get Tested

If you wake up with little or no recollection of the night before, it's quite possible there's more to the story than just a few too many pints. This is especially true if you wake up in a strange place or you feel as if you may have had sexual intercourse but can't remember.

Many date rape drugs only stay in the victim's system for a short period of time, so it is important to go to the hospital immediately to get tested. It is also essential that you refrain from showering or cleaning yourself, as this will make it difficult for hospital staff to conduct a rape examination, should you choose to have one done. You may also want to consider getting tested for sexually transmitted diseases, even if you are not certain if you engaged in sexual intercourse.

The All-Knowing Nail Polish

In 2014, four undergraduates at North Carolina State University developed a nail polish that changes color when it comes into contact with common date rape drugs like Rohypnol. There are also similar products like coasters, cups, and straws already on the market that work in a similar fashion.

■ Alert the Authorities

Whoever drugged you did so with malicious intent, and there's no way to know for certain what he or she is capable of doing. You should consider the person to be dangerous, and under no circumstances should you have any further contact.

While you may be angry and wish to do this person harm, not only would such actions put you at physical risk, they might also cause unnecessary legal trouble later on. Instead, alert the authorities to the situation and allow them to deal with your suspected attacker. While the process for bringing the person to justice may be a long and painful one, you may take comfort in the fact that your actions could protect others from having to go through the same process.

I've Stepped on a Nail

Likelihood of Happening: High
Ease of Prevention: Moderate
Is Time a Factor? No

All around the world, tens of thousands of discarded nails lie scattered on the ground, unremarkable and without purpose. What once may have held together a child's tree house or supported an old painting is now only good for one thing: ruining your day.

■ Decide How Bad It Is

While having a foreign object protruding from your foot is never a pleasant experience, it's rarely cause for serious concern. As long as the nail is not more than ½ inch in diameter and is not embedded more than ½ inch into your foot, you should be able to safely extract it yourself.

Puncture wounds don't normally result in serious bleeding, so if you do notice an abnormal amount of blood seeping from the wound, it is possible that the nail may have severed or nicked an artery. If you feel this may be the case, seek immediate medical attention and do not attempt to remove the nail, as it may actually be preventing blood loss.

■ Remove the Nail

Once you've decided that it's safe to remove the nail yourself, grab a pair of tweezers, a pair of latex gloves, some rubbing alcohol, and a bandage, and head to the bathroom to begin the extraction process. Before you get started, sanitize your tweezers either by boiling them in water for fifteen minutes or placing them in rubbing alcohol for the same period of time. Once they are sanitized, put on the pair of latex gloves and use the tweezers to firmly grasp the nail just below the head and gently maneuver it out of your foot. If the pain is too severe, take some over-the-counter pain medication and try again once it has taken effect.

Once the nail is safely out, allow the wound to bleed for a while to flush out any bacteria that the nail may have introduced. You can also use this time to inspect the area inside and around the wound for any metal shards or other debris that might have splintered off the nail. After approximately three minutes, apply pressure to stop the bleeding and clean the wound using a sterile saline solution—which can be purchased at any pharmacy—to ensure that no foreign bodies remain in the wound before you bandage it.

■ Get a Tetanus Shot

While you should watch your wound closely as it heals for signs of an infection, your immediate concern is avoiding tetanus. The disease, characterized by bone-breaking muscle spasms, can be fatal, especially to children and older adults. While most people in developed countries receive the tetanus vaccine routinely, its effectiveness does diminish over time. If it's been more than five years since you received a tetanus shot, you should go to the hospital and get a booster shot as soon as possible. Even if the nail appeared relatively clean, it's better to be safe than sorry.

Not Even Animals Are Safe

Shortly after his death, General Robert E. Lee's beloved horse Traveller had to be put down after he contracted tetanus from stepping on a nail.

I Cut Off My Finger

Likelihood of Happening: Low
Ease of Prevention: High
Is Time a Factor? Yes

Separating one of your digits from your hand is certainly no easy task, but that doesn't mean it's impossible. Whether you've injured yourself with a misplaced strike of a meat cleaver or a careless moment with a buzz saw, you're not alone; hospitals around the country deal with thousands of involuntary amputations every year. And while you can't turn back time to a few seconds before you chopped off your pinky, there are steps you can take to ensure a doctor will have a better chance of sewing it back on.

■ Stop the Bleeding

The moment you realize you are missing a finger—which shouldn't take long—either you or someone nearby should immediately call for an ambulance. When you know help is on the way, sit down and apply pressure directly to the site of the amputation, and elevate the affected hand. You can also lie down if sitting is uncomfortable, or if you feel you might faint. Only apply a tourniquet if the bleeding is so severe it could be life threatening. Too much pressure could damage the site and make reattachment more challenging later.

■ Preserve Your Finger

Once the bleeding is under control, track down your finger and gently rinse it off under cool running water. Your goal is to remove as much bacteria as possible, but be careful not to scrub too vigorously, as this could damage the delicate nerves. Next, wrap the finger in a damp cloth and place it into a sealed plastic bag. Do your best to trap a small amount of air in with the severed finger.

Finally, fill a bucket with cold water and a small amount of ice and place the sealed plastic bag inside. The air you left in the bag should allow the bag to float at the surface. Do not let the finger come into direct contact with the ice, as this could damage the blood vessels and make reattachment difficult. Despite what you may have seen on television or in movies, do not store the finger directly on ice, and do not place it in milk, alcohol, or any other liquid.

If You Have a Choice
In the unlikely event that you are losing your finger as a result of a hostage situation, don't go with the obvious choice and allow them to remove your pinky. Instead, go with the pointer finger on your nondominant hand. Your other fingers will adapt to the loss far better than if it were your pinky.

■ Keep Your Finger on Hand

When the ambulance arrives, make sure to alert them that you were able to recover the severed digit and you currently have it stored in cold water. Do not, under any circumstances, leave your finger with a friend or family member to take to the hospital. If they're delayed or if there's confusion at the hospital, you could lose valuable time and reattachment could become impossible. Instead, keep your finger with you at all times, from the moment you recover it to the moment you arrive at the hospital.

I'm about to Have a Car Accident

Likelihood of Happening: High
Ease of Prevention: High
Is Time a Factor? Yes

When you are out on the road, there are thousands of different ways you could find yourself in a traffic accident. Even traveling at the speed limit in the right-hand lane of an almost empty highway doesn't guarantee your safety, because another driver could easily fall asleep at the wheel next to you. While the fear of a collision shouldn't keep you from driving, it is important to be prepared should the unthinkable happen.

■ Brace for Impact

If an accident is unavoidable, you may have anywhere from an instant to a few seconds to prepare yourself for the collision. While it doesn't sound like much, it could be enough to save your life. If you have time, check out your:

- **Seat belt:** Make sure it is fastened securely across your waist and shoulder.
- **Posture:** Lean back in your seat and do your best to relax your body. Leaning forward could cause injury if the airbag deploys.
- **Stray Objects:** Even something as light as a laptop could become a deadly projectile in the event of a crash. If there's time, place any unsecured items on the floor of the passenger seat.

Most importantly, do your best to relax your body and accept the inevitable impact that is to come.

■ Stay Safe and Wait for Help to Arrive

If you have not suffered any major injuries, and your car is still operable, pull over to the side of the road to avoid causing a secondary accident. If your vehicle hasn't sustained significant damage, the safest thing to do is remain inside and call for assistance. Getting out could put you at unnecessary risk.

If there is significant damage to your car and you feel there may be danger of a fire, then immediately turn off the engine, exit your vehicle, retreat to a safe distance, and dial 911.

■ Survey the Damage

Once help arrives, you will have the chance to assess the damage to your vehicle and call your insurance company to begin the process of filing a claim. Take pictures of the vehicle as well as anything in the surrounding area that might have contributed to the crash. This could be anything from an upturned manhole cover that caused you to swerve, to a bush that obstructed a stop sign. The more information you have about the crash, the easier it will be for you to work with your insurance company to repair the damage to your vehicle.

I'm Developing Frostbite

- **Likelihood of Happening:** Moderate
- **Ease of Prevention:** High
- **Is Time a Factor?** Yes

We tend to associate frostbite with mountain climbers and skiers trapped in avalanches, but the truth is that it doesn't need to be −30°F to suffer from frostbite. In fact, it doesn't even need to be below 0°F to be at risk. With moderate winds, people have been known to exhibit symptoms of frostbite within just a few minutes of exposure to temperatures as high as 20°F. Even simple activities like shoveling your car out of the snow or walking your dog at night can put you in serious danger.

■ Know the Signs

When you are outside in winter, it's easy to write off the symptoms of frostbite as nothing to be concerned about. But if you don't address them quickly, they could result in very serious injury. Immediately head indoors if you experience numbness or a tingling sensation in your extremities; if your skin changes color to white, gray, yellow, or red; becomes hard; or takes on a waxy appearance. Similar to sunburn, frostbite occurs gradually in stages:

- **Frostnip:** The skin turns pale or red and becomes cold to the touch. You may experience pricking or numbness, but there should be no permanent damage.
- **Superficial Frostbite:** The skin may become hard, and may start to blister several days after exposure. Potential nerve damage may leave the area permanently numb to sensation.
- **Deep Frostbite:** The entire area freezes and damage extends beyond the skin to the muscle, tendons, and blood vessels underneath. In severe cases, amputation may be required to prevent gangrene.

The longer you ignore the symptoms, the greater the risk that the severity of the frostbite will increase.

■ Treat the Injury

If you believe you are suffering from superficial or deep frostbite, you should seek immediate medical attention. However, there are some steps you can take on the way to the hospital or while waiting for an ambulance that could improve your prognosis.

First, gradually warm the affected area by placing the damaged skin against the body—such as cupping your hands inside your armpits—or submerging the area in warm water between 100 and 108°F. Avoid direct heat sources like heating pads or stovetops, as they can cause burns. If possible, also avoid walking on frostbitten feet or toes, as this could further damage the area. You may experience considerable pain as blood flow returns to the area and it begins to thaw. Take over-the-counter pain medication to help alleviate some of the discomfort.

Once you make it to the hospital, a doctor may continue to rewarm the skin and wrap the area in sterile gauze. The doctor may also need to remove some damaged tissue, which could require months of observation to determine the extent of the injury. This could be limited to a small amount of skin, or could require amputation of entire limbs, so prepare yourself for any outcome.

I'm in a Bar Fight

- **Likelihood of Happening:** Moderate
- **Ease of Prevention:** High
- **Is Time a Factor?** No

Most people go to a bar because they are looking to have a few drinks and share a few laughs with friends. Others are there to meet Mr. or

Ms. Right—or at least a temporary placeholder. But every now and then you come across people who seem to be only interested in downing shots and kicking ass . . . and they're all out of money for shots.

■ Beat Your Opponent to the Punch

Your best option is to play the diplomat and calm everyone down, but if you think confrontation is inevitable, you want to make sure to land the first punch. A single quick punch to the face could be enough to send the aggressive bar patron to the floor, or at least to the bathroom to deal with a bloody nose. At the very least, it will catch your opponent off guard and tip the scales immediately in your favor.

While you are more likely to connect with a short jab, a right or left hook has a higher chance of knocking your opponent unconscious, which is sure to end the fight immediately. If you feel your opponent is too inebriated to dodge a slow, powerful right hook, then this might be the best strategy.

■ Stay on Your Feet

If you aren't able to end the altercation quickly, your primary goal is to remain on your feet. If you trip or are knocked to the ground, you risk being kicked or pinned down by the weight of your opponent. If you do wind up on the floor, do your best to protect your head until you are able to stand up again.

Be aware of your surroundings, and keep an eye out for anyone who might attempt to jump in and join the fray. If possible, keep your back to a nearby wall at all times. If anyone else does join the fight in defense of your opponent, immediately make a break for it. Fighting two people simultaneously is simply too dangerous.

■ Keep Up the Attack

Unless your opponent is unconscious or has left the premises, there's still an immediate threat to your safety. Keep up your assault until your opponent is completely incapacitated. When you aren't attacking, maintain a safe distance until you intend to strike. This keeps you out of your opponent's strike zone and lets you control the pace of the fight.

When you do strike, aim for vulnerable areas like the face, throat, chest, and kidneys. Remember, this is a fight to protect yourself, not a boxing match; don't be afraid to fight dirty by aiming for the eyes or going in for a head butt. Luckily, in most cases a bouncer will break up the fight or the police will be called shortly after it begins, so you won't have to bob and weave for long.

I Have a Nasty Sunburn

- **Likelihood of Happening:** High
- **Ease of Prevention:** High
- **Is Time a Factor?** No

The days when hordes of sunbathers slathered their bodies with tanning oil and baked on the beach for hours are behind us. Nowadays, foil sun reflectors have been replaced with beach umbrellas, and you'll be lucky to find a bottle of sunscreen below an SPF 30 rating. But despite the precautions, it's still possible to fall victim to a particularly gruesome sunburn.

■ Get Indoors and Stay There

Symptoms of sunburn can begin as soon as two to four hours after exposure, but they may not reach their peak until many hours later. So what initially appears to be a minor issue can escalate to a very painful burn if you continue to expose yourself to the sun's harmful rays. With that in mind, seek shelter as soon as you notice any significant reddening of the skin, and avoid further exposure for the remainder of the day. You should be able to determine the severity of the burn within around twenty-four hours of exposure.

■ Treat the Burn

Sunburns are categorized in the same way other burns are classified. A first-degree sunburn will turn the skin slightly pink, and cause mild inflammation and discomfort. Second-degree sunburns are characterized by blistering and subsequent peeling of the skin. Fortunately, there haven't been any documented cases of a third-degree sunburn.

For mild burns, treat the pain and inflammation with an over-the-counter pain reliever containing ibuprofen. Hydrocortisone creams and hydrating lotions containing aloe vera may also help reduce the swelling. If the burn site feels warm to the touch, take a cold shower or apply cool compresses to get some relief.

For more serious burns that exhibit blisters, extra care should be taken to ensure a secondary infection does not occur. Trim away any dead skin from broken blisters and immediately apply antibacterial cream to the area. Drink plenty of water to avoid dehydration.

■ Protect Yourself

Most of the pain associated with a sunburn will subside within two to three days from the start of symptoms. As your skin heals, you may experience significant peeling and find the skin underneath is particularly sensitive. Applying moisturizing lotion to the area can help mitigate this problem. You should also take special care in the days and weeks that follow to cover the healing skin when outdoors.

Repeated sunburns can increase your risk for skin cancer and other skin disorders, so it's important that you remember to apply sunscreen with a rating of at least SPF 30 when outdoors for extended periods, and to wear protective clothing. In order to adequately cover an average adult male body with sunscreen, a single application should consist of approximately one ounce of lotion. Don't forget to apply sunscreen directly behind the ears and use a lip balm with SPF.

I've Been Working in Poison Ivy

- **Likelihood of Happening:** Moderate
- **Ease of Prevention:** Moderate
- **Is Time a Factor?** No

There's nothing like an afternoon spent working outside to give you a sense of accomplishment. With all the weed pulling and branch trimming, it's unlikely you pay much attention to what type of plants you are clearing off your property. And most of the time it's not an issue. That is until you go to throw away your bag of yard trimmings and notice an abundance of poison ivy staring up at you.

■ Act Fast

Poison ivy, as well as poison oak and poison sumac, secrete a poisonous substance called urushiol. Unless you are one of the lucky 15 percent of the population who are immune to the oil's effects, you will start to develop an unpleasant oozing rash on any exposed skin within twenty-four hours. If you act quickly, however, you might be able to spare yourself that uncomfortable fate.

Within ten minutes of exposure, as much as 50 percent of the urushiol has already penetrated the skin, which makes it imperative that you wash the affected area with soap and water as soon as you think you may have come in contact with poison ivy. Even if several hours have passed, you should still thoroughly wash any affected skin to reduce the severity of the reaction.

You also want to wash any clothing or gardening equipment with laundry detergent or a commercial poison ivy cleanser. Despite the popular myth that touching a poison ivy rash can spread it from person to person or from one area of the body to another, the rash itself is not contagious. The oil that causes the rash, however, can remain active on clothing and other objects for several years. Wear gloves when cleaning off the oil, and try not to let any contaminated gear come into contact with your skin.

■ Treat the Rash

If you weren't able to remove all of the urushiol in time, you'll start to notice bumpy red spots wherever the plant made contact with your skin. While they can be painful and itchy, do your best not to scratch them, as this can cause a secondary infection. Instead, you can ease discomfort by taking frequent baths in a lukewarm colloidal oatmeal preparation. Calamine lotion, hydrocortisone cream, and over-the-counter oral antihistamines can also be effective at managing the unpleasant itching. You might also find that a cool compress provides temporary relief.

For severe reactions, especially those around the face and eyes, a doctor may prescribe an oral steroid that should relieve all symptoms in a matter of days.

I Get Jalapeño Oil in My Eyes

Likelihood of Happening: Moderate
Ease of Prevention: High
Is Time a Factor? No

Spicy jalapeño peppers can add a delightful kick of heat to everything from nachos and chili to sandwiches, and even ice cream. The spicy flavor and moderate burning sensation comes from a waxy compound in the pepper known as capsaicin. Even if you are unfamiliar with capsaicin, you are likely familiar with the pleasant burning sensation it causes in the mouth. What you might not have known before—but are now realizing as you claw at your face and writhe around on the floor—is that capsaicin causes a similar burning sensation in other parts of the body as well. Especially soft tissues, like the eyes.

■ Find Relief

The good news is that the uncomfortable burning sensation you are experiencing is not permanent. Given enough time, your body will naturally rid itself of the capsaicin without any lasting damage to your eyes. Luckily, you can speed this process along by pouring one of several different liquids into a shot glass, pressing the rim against your eyelid to create a seal, and tipping the glass back into your open eye. These liquids include:

- **Milk:** Proteins found in milk called casein help breakdown the capsaicin and can provide near-instant relief.

- **Saline Solution:** This mimics your body's natural tears and will help to flush the painful capsaicin out of your eyes.
- **Water:** Capsaicin is not particularly water soluble, so neither this method nor saline will be as effective as milk. However, repeatedly flushing your eyes with cold water can help to relieve the burning sensation.

One application of any of these treatments may not be enough to provide necessary relief. If you are still in considerable pain, repeat the process until the pain subsides.

■ Protect Yourself Next Time

Now that you've experienced the painful reality of touching your eyes after chopping jalapeños, it's unlikely it's something you'd like to try again soon. To avoid a repeat performance, wear latex gloves whenever you handle this pepper, especially the white inner pith, which contains the highest concentrations of capsaicin.

The Weaponization of Peppers

Capsaicin is a common ingredient in the pepper sprays used by law enforcement to disperse crowds and safely immobilize individuals deemed to be a threat. The intensity of the spray can vary from around 500,000 Scoville heat units to as high as 5,000,000. By comparison, a habanero pepper is usually ranked between 100,000 and 350,000 Scoville units, while the infamous bhut jolokia (a.k.a the ghost chile) can be upwards of 1,000,000 Scoville units.

If you prefer not to wear gloves, rinse your hands with vegetable oil followed by soap and water before you touch any exposed skin.

Capsaicin is more soluble in oil than water, so the oil will be more effective at removing it than soap and water alone.

I Hit My Head

- **Likelihood of Happening:** High
- **Ease of Prevention:** Low
- **Is Time a Factor?** Yes

Humans generally go to a lot of trouble to protect their heads, and with good reason. While our bodies are able to bounce back from various cuts, punctures, fractures, and burns with relative ease, injuries to the brain are not as easy to shrug off. While not all head injuries are life threatening, any blow to the cranium should be taken very seriously.

■ Decide If You Need Medical Assistance

Whether you've slipped on a patch of ice or a poorly hit golf ball slammed straight into your forehead, you should immediately dial 911 if you experience any of the following:

- Loss of consciousness
- Headache
- Memory loss
- Confusion
- Changes to vision
- Trouble staying awake
- Unequal pupil size
- Vomiting

If you are not experiencing any of these symptoms, treat the injury by applying ice to the impact site and administering over-the-counter pain medication. Keep in mind, however, that even a brief period of unconsciousness is cause to seek medical attention.

■ Begin Preliminary Treatment

In the event of a significant head injury, it is important that you move your head, neck, and back as little as possible while you wait for the ambulance to arrive, as you could have also injured your neck or spinal column. If you are already on the ground, do not attempt to stand up. Instead, lie prone on your back.

Even minor head injuries can cause significant bleeding, which you can address by applying firm pressure to the area with a clean piece of cloth. If you suspect your skull may have been fractured, simply cover the wound with sterile dressing and do not apply any pressure.

If you feel the need to vomit, gently roll your entire body so that you are on your side when you do so. This will help prevent you from choking.

■ Continue to Monitor Yourself

The doctors at the hospital will be able to determine whether you've experienced any significant brain trauma, but it could take weeks or months to discover if you will suffer any long-term effects. Some warning signs to look out for include:

- Persistent pain in the head or neck
- Chronic headaches
- Amnesia

- Trouble concentrating
- Disorientation
- Fluid or blood leaking from the nose
- Tinnitus (ringing in the ears)
- Slurred speech
- Trouble sleeping
- Blurred vision
- Sensitivity to light
- Seizures

If you experience any of these symptoms, immediately alert your doctor.

You should be able to take acetaminophen for any pain, but avoid taking ibuprofen unless directed otherwise by your doctor. You should also avoid alcohol for the duration of your recovery.

I Break My Nose

Likelihood of Happening: High
Ease of Prevention: Moderate
Is Time a Factor? No

Of all our appendages, few are as vulnerable to trauma as the humble nose. As the most bulbous portion of our face, it often receives the initial force of any wayward footballs or other poorly thrown objects. And while it may be relatively sturdy, all things considered, there's only so much abuse a nose can take before it breaks.

■ Stop the Bleeding

In the aftermath of a fractured nose, it is quite common to experience a significant amount of bleeding. While conventional wisdom states you should pinch your nose shut and tilt your head back to stem the flow, you should actually avoid this practice. Doing so could cause blood to spill down the back of your throat, resulting in vomiting. Instead pinch your nose with your thumb and forefinger and tilt your head forward.

Once the bleeding stops, which should take approximately ten to twenty minutes, apply an ice pack to the area to reduce the swelling. Severe swelling is common, so don't be alarmed.

■ Try to Treat It at Home . . .

Provided the injury is not serious, you can treat the fracture yourself by applying ice packs and keeping the head elevated at night to reduce swelling. While your nostrils may become blocked after the injury, you should avoid blowing your nose, as doing so could aggravate the injury and cause further bleeding. If you are experiencing considerable pain, you can take over-the-counter acetaminophen, but you should avoid taking ibuprofen which could actually increase the bleeding.

■ . . . Or Go to the Hospital

Most nose fractures are not serious and will heal on their own without any professional medical intervention. However, you should go to the hospital if:

- You continue to bleed uncontrollably
- Your nose is crooked or bent at an odd angle
- You are experiencing clear drainage from one or both nostrils
- There is localized swelling near the septum

Immediately after the fracture, a doctor may be able to realign your nose without the need for surgery. But if the injury took place some time ago, or the break is particularly severe, surgery may be necessary to repair the damage. The doctor may even send you home for a few days to allow time for the swelling to subside so he can better assess the situation when you return.

If you are experiencing uncontrollable bleeding, the doctor may pack your nose with gauze. He may also need to make a small incision near your septum to allow a blood clot to drain.

I Break My Leg Hiking

Likelihood of Happening: Moderate
Ease of Prevention: Moderate
Is Time a Factor? Yes

There is no good place to break your leg, but some locations are certainly better than others. Outside of a hospital during an orthopedic surgeon convention, for example, isn't all that bad in the grand scheme of things. On the other hand, at the top of a mountain, miles away from civilization . . . not nearly as good.

■ Stop Moving and Start Thinking

The moment you think you might be injured, put yourself in a position that temporarily immobilizes the affected limb. If you've suffered a fractured bone, there might be sharp edges that could sever an artery and cause internal bleeding. There's also risk for other internal injuries, such as damage to muscle tissue and tendons, so the less you move the leg, the better.

To stabilize your broken leg, place two thick sticks along the left and right sides of your broken leg. Using paracord, handkerchiefs, or even pieces of torn clothing, tie the sticks to your limb at regular intervals. Just be sure not to place them too close to the fracture, or tie them so tight that they restrict blood flow. These makeshift splints will ensure your leg remains relatively immobile.

If you have walkie-talkies or a cell phone, use them immediately to call for help. If you can't get reception or you don't have a way to communicate with the outside world, send somebody ahead to get help while you wait patiently with the rest of your party. If you are hiking solo, then things are a little more complicated. If it's early in the day, or you have enough supplies to make it through the night, then your best bet right now is to hunker down and wait for another hiker to pass by. If you don't have the gear or clothing to survive a night in the wilderness, however, you are going to need to hike out with a broken leg. If this is the case, take stock of any tools and items you have at your disposal that might help you get out of this mess.

■ Stay Slow and Steady

As with all unexpected disasters, your greatest asset is your ability to remain calm. If you panic and rush, you will only succeed in injuring yourself further.

If you have hiking poles, use them to stabilize yourself as you move. You can also find Y-shaped branches to use as makeshift crutches, but make sure they're strong enough to not break under your weight. Take slow, deliberate steps and pay close attention to the terrain so you don't slip and fall.

As you make your way back to civilization, focus on achieving small, simple goals so you don't become overwhelmed by the enormity of the task at hand. If you can make it ten yards to that rock up ahead, you can surely make it to that tree off in the distance. If you can make it to that tree, you can make it back to the bridge you saw a mile back. And if you can make it that far, you can make it back to the highway and to safety.

I Threw My Back Out

- **Likelihood of Happening:** Moderate
- **Ease of Prevention:** Moderate
- **Is Time a Factor?** No

When you are young, you feel invincible and may say seemingly ridiculous things like, "Of course I can lift that fifty-pound bag of fertilizer for you, ma'am. Where would you like it?" As you age, however, even simple tasks like bending down to pick up the TV remote off the floor can be enough to leave you squealing in pain, clutching your back, and looking for a place to sit down. One of the luxuries of being old, though, is you have an excuse to actually treat the problem instead of shrugging it off like it's no big deal.

■ Admit Defeat

Whether you are in the middle of moving a heavy piece of furniture, or you simply twisted your back oddly while playing tennis, just go ahead and admit that you are done with physical activity for the day. If you keep straining yourself, you may cause even more damage to the affected area.

Instead, find a nice open spot on the ground and lie down flat on your stomach, with your arms at your side. A bed or couch might be more comfortable, but you really want a rigid surface. Allow your body to relax, and place a towel under your forehead so you can breathe normally without turning your head.

■ Reduce Pain and Swelling

When you strain your muscles, your body's immediate reaction is to send blood to the area. Unfortunately, too much inflammation can lengthen the recovery process. To combat the pain and swelling, take an over-the-counter analgesic such as ibuprofen or acetaminophen and apply ice immediately after the injury. Wrap the ice in a towel and apply it directly to the affected area for no longer than fifteen minutes at a time. Wait at least an hour between applications.

For at least the first two days—preferably three—stick exclusively to ice and avoid heating pads or hot showers. While heat may feel like it's helping, it actually increases the blood flow to the area and just makes things worse.

■ Don't Become a Couch Potato

Conventional wisdom holds that you should lie in bed for the next few days until your back feels better, but recent studies have actually found that you will recover more quickly if you resume moderate activity as soon as you are able.

After a few days of rest, slowly build back up to your usual routine. You should continue to avoid any strenuous exercise for a few weeks, but simple activities like walking to the store or doing chores around the house can be very helpful for the recovery process.

I Get Doored on My Bike

Likelihood of Happening: High
Ease of Prevention: Moderate
Is Time a Factor? No

In most areas of the United States, cyclists find themselves traveling in areas that are not particularly safe for them. And while all bikers are highly attuned to the dangers of the cars swerving around them, it turns out that you really need to watch out for the cars that aren't moving at all: Without warning, a careless driver or passenger can send you flying to the pavement by simply opening a door.

■ Plan for Impact

In the few milliseconds between when you notice the open door and you collide with it, repeat the following phrase to yourself: "I will fall toward the car. I will not fall into traffic."

Ramming into an open car door at 20 mph is sure to cause injury, but if you are thrown out into the street it's quite possible you could be struck—or worse, run over—by a passing motorist. If you can, lean back on your seat, apply the brakes, and angle your front tire toward the car, rather than away from it. While your gut reaction will be to swerve away from the door, this can be extremely dangerous if you don't have time to look over your shoulder first. In this case, it's better to be alive and in pain than dead.

■ Remain Seated

As with any major bicycle accident, spinal cord injuries are a very serious risk. Even less serious complications like broken bones or strained muscles can be exacerbated by sudden movements. Immediately after the collision, stay still on the ground for a few moments to compose yourself and assess the damage done to your body. If your extremities are numb or you're unable to move your legs, then stay still until help arrives.

If you do not believe you are seriously injured, slowly move yourself to the side of the road to sit down. Even if you feel fine, you could have internal injuries and it is best if you don't walk around.

■ Call an Ambulance and the Police—in That Order

Unless the accident was at very low speed, you need to call an ambulance to take you to the hospital and ensure you do not have any serious injuries. Once help is on the way, call the police and ask them to come to the scene to take a statement.

A lot of drivers and onlookers will try to dissuade you from calling the police and may even place blame on you, but the important thing to remember is that it is irrelevant who caused the accident. Calling the police ensures that there will be documentation of the accident, should you need to file an insurance claim later.

I Think I'm Being Followed

Likelihood of Happening: Low
Ease of Prevention: Low
Is Time a Factor? No

Whether you are driving on a deserted country road or walking home from the bar late at night, the last thing you want to experience is that sinking feeling you get when you sense you are being followed. Sure, it could be nothing more than your imagination getting the best of you, but it's better to be safe than sorry.

◾ Don't Let on That You Suspect

Assuming you are actually being followed, you don't want to draw attention to the fact that you know. If they realize you are onto them, they might jump into action if they are looking for a fight or are out to take your wallet.

Keep walking or driving at your normal pace and resist the urge to look over your shoulder every few seconds. Once you feel comfortable, stop to tie your shoe or slow down in your car to see if anyone else in the vicinity does the same. Making four turns in the same direction is another surefire way to determine if someone is following you, but it will also tip them off that you are suspicious, so be careful if attempting this maneuver.

Keep a Lookout for Shoes

In the off chance you are being tailed by professionals, it's possible there is a whole team of people following your every move who are constantly altering their appearance to throw you off. Shoes, however, are articles of clothing that are difficult to change on the fly, and can be a good indicator of whether the casual guy in jeans and a T-shirt is actually the same man who ran past you in track pants a few minutes ago.

◾ Head for a Police Station

Whether you are in a car or on foot, under no circumstances should you attempt to confront the individual yourself or slow down to let them overtake you. If you are familiar with the area, continue to play it cool and head toward the local police station.

If you are on foot and you can't walk that far safely, start moving toward a public place like a restaurant or a coffee shop so you can call the police from there. Don't stop to make a call on your cell phone; just keep walking and act normally. Once you are safely shielded by restaurant diners or boisterous bar patrons, keep an eye out for your pursuer and make a mental note of any defining characteristics. This will help police track him down later.

I Am Stung by a Jellyfish

- **Likelihood of Happening:** Low
- **Ease of Prevention:** Low
- **Is Time a Factor?** Yes

The beach can be a wonderful, relaxing place with the sun shining, the cool breeze whipping off the crisp ocean water, and attentive resort staff supplying you with an endless supply of frozen drinks with umbrellas sticking out of them. Of course, it's a little difficult to enjoy the scenery when your leg feels like it's been dipped in battery acid.

■ Get to Shore

If you're in the ocean and you think you've been stung by a jellyfish, your first course of action is to make your way out of the water. If there are still jellyfish in the area, you will want to do your best to avoid them on your way to shore. Once on dry land, refrain from touching the affected area as much as possible. The tentacles present on the skin may contain nematocysts, the poisonous barbs from the jellyfish tentacles, and touching them could cause further damage.

■ Remove the Tentacles

The number of folk remedies for jellyfish stings range from the plausible (baking soda) to the absurd (urine), but few of them provide any significant relief if you've been stung. While vinegar was the suggested treatment for some time, most medical professionals now recommend warm seawater to rinse off as many of the attached nematocysts as possible. The warm water will also help to soothe some of the discomfort.

Next, track down a pair of gloves to protect your hands and use tweezers to carefully remove any tentacles that may be present on the skin. If you don't have tweezers, a credit card or even a stick scraped along the skin will suffice so long as you are careful. Try your best to keep still while you remove the tentacles, as you could inadvertently cause attached nematocysts to fire and make the situation worse.

Once you've rid yourself of as many visible tentacles as possible, soak the affected area in warm water for a period of thirty minutes both to soothe the skin and to remove any final stray tentacle remnants.

■ Deal with the Aftermath

The pain caused by a jellyfish sting will generally subside within a few hours, but there are some species that can cause welts that linger for a number of days. If you experience any discomfort, treat it with over-the-counter pain relievers and ice packs. Any open sores, rashes, or burns should be treated with antibiotic ointment to prevent infection.

To be safe, it is also advisable that you discard any items that may have come into contact with nematocysts, such as your swimsuit and beach towel. The venomous structures can remain intact for several days, and can continue to cause you harm.

I Have the World's Worst Hangover

- **Likelihood of Happening:** High
- **Ease of Prevention:** High
- **Is Time a Factor?** No

It started out harmlessly enough. Your coworkers wanted to grab a beer after work, which turned into four. Then the bar down the street had five-dollar Long Island Iced Teas—of which you drank three—and when you got home, you uttered the famous last words, "One more isn't going to kill me." Now it's 7:00 A.M., your head is pounding, and you wish that last drink *had* done you in, because now you feel horrible.

■ Avoid the Coffee, Stick with Water

The idea that coffee will help sober you up after a night of heavy drinking is antiquated, and will actually do more harm than good. Caffeine is a diuretic and could contribute to dehydration. Instead, opt for good old-fashioned water, or possibly a sugary sports drink if your stomach is feeling up to it.

As you hydrate, consider popping some ibuprofen to help with that pounding headache you are almost certainly experiencing. Just stay clear of any painkillers containing acetaminophen, as they can be harmful to the liver when combined with the alcohol still lingering in your system.

■ Be Gentle on Your Stomach

Even if food is the last thing on your mind, you might want to rummage around in the bread drawer and make yourself some dry toast. While the notion that the carbon in toast can filter out "toxins" is a myth, the bland bread itself should help settle your stomach and stabilize your blood sugar. Some other good options are bananas (to replenish potassium), eggs (to provide calories), fruit juice (to boost energy and provide vitamins), and chicken broth (to restore salt).

■ Admit Defeat and Go Back to Bed

There's a reason you can sleep for ten hours after a night out and still feel exhausted. Overindulging in alcohol can prevent you from slipping into REM—Rapid Eye Movement—sleep throughout the course of the night. These phases occur at regular intervals throughout the night, and individuals who are unable to achieve periods of REM sleep often report feeling less refreshed the following day. Don't fight your body's natural desire to achieve normal, uninterrupted sleep. Instead, call in sick to work, fall back into bed, and consider taking it a little easier next time.

I Spill Hot Coffee on Myself

Likelihood of Happening: Moderate
Ease of Prevention: High
Is Time a Factor? No

When 79-year-old Stella Liebeck spilled a hot cup of McDonald's coffee on herself in 1994, she became the butt of countless jokes at her expense. People called the ensuing lawsuit frivolous, questioning how much damage a cup of coffee could possibly cause. As it turns out, a lot.

Liebeck suffered third-degree burns to her pelvic region and had to undergo painful skin graft treatments and years of rehabilitation. Despite the lawsuit, the fast food giant has not reduced the temperature and continues to serve their coffee between 176–194°F, so a freshly brewed cup of joe is still a potential hazard.

■ Get It Off Your Skin

While you will instinctively wipe any hot liquid off of your exposed skin, saturated clothing can continue to burn you if you don't remove it quickly. Be careful, though; you could inadvertently rip off portions of your epidermis that have attached to your clothing. If you feel your skin sticking to your clothes, leave them on.

Once you get your clothes off, immediately run cold water over any burnt skin and surrounding areas for at least fifteen minutes. This will ease the pain, and also stop the burn from getting worse.

■ Cover the Affected Area

Burn sites are very prone to infection and irritation. To prevent this, cover the area with plastic wrap, gauze, or a cool, damp cloth. Avoid using ice packs, as the burn makes the skin more susceptible to frostbite.

Blistering skin is a sign of a more serious burn and means that you should seek medical treatment. You should also head to the emergency room if the affected area is roughly more than 1 percent of your total body mass (approximately the size of your palm).

■ Treat the Pain and Swelling

Even minor burns can be very painful, both immediately after the incident and as the body heals. Over-the-counter medications like ibuprofen can help treat the pain, as well as reduce swelling. Avoid applying any ointments directly to the burn site, however, unless they were prescribed by a physician. Elevating the area of the burn can also help by reducing swelling, provided this does not cause you additional discomfort.

The pain caused by first-degree burns should subside within a matter of days, but second-degree burns may still be painful several weeks after the incident. Third-degree burns might require skin grafting as well as antibiotics to prevent infection, and should be treated by a medical professional.

I Cut Myself While Cooking

Likelihood of Happening: High
Ease of Prevention: High
Is Time a Factor? No

Your chef's knife is your single most versatile kitchen tool. It can make short work of thick slabs of meat and even chop through thin chicken bones, but it's also precise enough to finely mince garlic or thinly slice a tomato. Unfortunately, its cutting prowess isn't discriminatory, and it will just as happily slice your hand as it will an onion.

■ Calm Down and Check the Wound

The sight of blood can be scary for those unaccustomed to it, especially when it's pouring out of your own body. The good news is that even a severe kitchen injury is very treatable, and you are going to be just fine.

Before you do anything, check to see if the cut is oozing or squirting. If blood squirts out of the wound intermittently, then you may have nicked an artery and should seek immediate medical attention. If not, then you should be able to treat the issue yourself.

■ Worry about Infection First, Bleeding Second

There's a reason you are supposed to wash your hands after you handle raw meat, especially chicken and ground beef: The surface is often crawling with harmful bacteria. With that in mind—assuming that you've determined that your wound is treatable at home—you need to thoroughly wash the cut with antibacterial soap and water.

Once the cut is thoroughly cleaned, take a look at the damage. If you've managed to inflict a cut longer than ⅔ of an inch, or you can see through to muscle tissue or bone, you may need to head to the hospital for stitches. If not, grab a clean towel and apply firm pressure directly to the wound. If possible, raise the affected area above your heart for around fifteen minutes, or longer if the bleeding hasn't stopped.

■ Grab the First-Aid Kit

Even though you've sanitized the cut, infection is still a genuine concern. Before you apply a bandage, you'll want to smear antibiotic ointment over the affected area. Depending on the size of the cut, a simple bandage should suffice, but for larger lacerations a gauze pad may better cover the area.

Don't panic if blood soaks through the bandage after you've applied it. Even simple movements can cause the cut to reopen and blood to seep. Just remove the bandage and replace it with a new one until the bleeding stops. If you have to replace the bandage several times within an hour, however, you may need to head to the hospital.

■ Take Care of Secondary Dangers

If you were in the middle of cooking, there are a number of possible safety hazards you may have been ignoring while treating your injury. Now that you have the bleeding under control, make sure to turn off any burners, remove anything from the oven that could catch fire, and throw away any food that might have been exposed to blood. You will also want to decontaminate your counters and other surfaces where blood may have splattered. And, while you may feel perfectly comfortable finishing up dinner, do yourself a favor and order some pizza.

I Encounter a Stray Dog

Likelihood of Happening: Moderate
Ease of Prevention: Moderate
Is Time a Factor? No

Selective breeding of man's best friend has given rise to everything from the six-pound Chihuahua to the 200-pound English Mastiff—and everything in between. While a chance encounter with a stray Pomeranian is nothing to be worried about, a larger, more aggressive canine is a lot more concerning.

■ Be Cautious

Whether you've grown up with dogs your entire life or you've had a significant fear since childhood, it's important to approach any encounter with caution. If you come across an off-leash dog, your immediate goal is to stop moving and assess the situation.

First and foremost, avoid making eye contact with the animal, as this can be interpreted as an act of aggression. Next, from a safe distance, check if the dog has a collar to determine if you are dealing with a lost pet or a stray. Keep in mind that even if the dog does appear to have a home, you should still tread lightly. You could inadvertently provoke an attack if the animal is injured or feels threatened.

Next, pay close attention to the animal's demeanor. Subtle clues like a raised tail and ears as well as bared teeth are sure signs that the animal is aggressive and might attack if approached. Barking is another clear indicator that the dog doesn't want you to get any closer than you already are. Folded-back ears and a tail that is tucked down could indicate the dog is frightened.

■ Plan Your Exit Strategy

As you are sizing up the dog, you can rest assured it is paying very close attention to you as well. Your best bet is to slowly back away from the animal and retreat to a safe distance to call animal control. Resist the urge to run, as this can trigger the dog to attack and it will almost certainly be able to outrun you.

If the animal does start coming toward you, seek higher ground like the roof of a car, a small tree, or anything tall enough that would prevent it from getting to you. If you have no means of escape, however, you may need to defend yourself.

■ Treat the Encounter Like a Fight for Your Life

Harming a stray dog may be difficult for some—especially animal lovers—but you have every right to protect yourself if you are attacked.

As the dog approaches, search your environment for anything you can use as a weapon or a shield to keep the dog at bay. Large sticks and rocks can be used to attack the animal while you employ a purse, backpack, or rolled-up sweater to protect your body. If you have nothing else available, you can offer the dog your nondominant arm to distract it while you use your stronger arm to strike at its most vulnerable areas—the eyes, neck, and jaws—until you disable the animal or help arrives.

Dog Attacks Are Rarely Fatal

Dogs bite more than four million Americans each year, but of those only about 19 (or around 0.0002 percent) are fatal. That number is exclusive to dog bites, and does not include deaths caused by secondary infection resulting from a dog bite. In the majority of fatal attacks, the victims are children under ten years old.

I Get Food Poisoning

Likelihood of Happening: Moderate
Ease of Prevention: Moderate
Is Time a Factor? No

Food poisoning is great when it's used as a fake excuse to take a day off from work. When it's actually a food-borne illness and not just a case of the Mondays, however, it's definitely not as fun.

The Centers for Disease Control and Prevention estimates that as many as one in six Americans suffer from some form of food-borne illness every year. Of those, 128,000 will be hospitalized and 3,000 will die as a result. While it's true the vast majority of those afflicted survive the ordeal, any form of food poisoning should be taken very seriously.

■ Drink Plenty of Fluids

If you are vomiting excessively and experiencing frequent bouts of diarrhea, you run the risk of dehydration if you don't replenish the fluids you lose every time you take a trip to the bathroom. Stick to clear liquids like water or juice, and avoid those with caffeine or alcohol. If you can manage to keep them down, sports drinks can be particularly beneficial since they will replace the electrolytes you have been losing. Chicken or beef broth is also a good option, as it will provide you with a few calories in addition to helping you stay hydrated.

■ Rest Up

While it's unlikely that you are going to suddenly feel motivated to run a marathon when you are stricken with food poisoning, you should really steer clear of anything even remotely resembling strenuous activity. Sweating will deplete your body of precious moisture, causing you to become dehydrated, and physical exertion could exacerbate your other symptoms.

Instead, find a cool, dimly lit room and lie down in whatever position makes you feel most comfortable. If you do manage to doze off, make sure you have a trash bin handy in case you wake suddenly due to a fit of nausea.

■ Take It Slow with Food

When you do finally feel comfortable eating food—which can take several hours or even upwards of two days—resist the temptation to scarf down an entire hamburger right away. Instead, focus on eating small bites of simple, basic food at regular intervals. Many doctors recommend the BRAT diet for those recovering from food poisoning, which consists of bananas, rice, applesauce, and toast.

▓ Head to the Hospital Now

While most instances of food poisoning are mild, more severe cases can require a trip to the emergency room. If you experience any of the following, it would be wise to head straight for the hospital:

- Dizziness
- High fever (above 104°F)
- Dehydration
- Irrepressible diarrhea or vomiting
- Lesions or discoloration of the skin

While the effects of food poisoning can be embarrassing for some, there is serious risk of death if you let your pride get in the way of receiving appropriate medical care.

CHAPTER 3

Expensive Mishaps You Wish Had Never Happened

It's true that accidents are a natural part of life, but why do they always seem to happen around expensive things? You could have the same wallet for fifteen years, but the moment you decide to take $1,000 out of the ATM it mysteriously grows legs and wanders off. The unfortunate reality is you can't turn back the clock and undo every expensive mistake you've made in your life, but thankfully, there are steps you can take to mitigate the damage.

I'm Drowning in Credit Card Debt

— **Likelihood of Happening:** Moderate
— **Ease of Prevention:** High
— **Is Time a Factor?** Yes

Credit cards are incredibly useful tools that allow us to make large purchases without carrying around briefcases full of cash. They also provide a simple way to keep track of spending habits and many provide customers with incentive bonuses every time they're used. However, credit cards also make it easy for individuals to fall quickly into considerable debt.

■ Do the Math

Many people with serious credit card debt purposely avoid evaluating the extent of the problem because it makes them upset to think about it. If you want to get yourself out of debt, you will need to attack the problem head on and stop avoiding it.

Start by going through your credit card and bank statements and take note of all the areas you are spending money. To keep things simple, lump each purchase into one of two categories: essential or nonessential. Things like gas, groceries, and medical costs should be considered essential, while restaurants, movies, and gifts would fall into the nonessential category. Once you know where your money is going, weigh it against the money you have coming in, and figure out where you can make cuts. You don't necessarily need to start living exclusively on ramen noodles and hot dogs, but perhaps you can start bringing lunch to work instead of eating out. If you're already down to a bare-bones existence, consider getting a second job to increase your income.

■ Negotiate with Your Creditors

Depending on the size of your debt, how much of it you've already paid, how long it's been since you've made a payment, and a host of other factors, you may be able to significantly reduce the amount you owe. You can either discuss the matter with the credit card companies directly, or you can turn to any one of a number of private companies that will help you with the negotiations.

If the interest you are currently paying is more of an issue than the amount you owe, consider calling your credit card company to request a rate reduction. While such an adjustment might come with stipulations, and there's no guarantee that the customer service rep will be able to help you, it certainly never hurts to try.

■ File for Bankruptcy

In extreme circumstances, your only option may be to file for bankruptcy to eliminate your debt. Before you do so, however, make sure you have thoroughly evaluated all other options and spoken with a bankruptcy lawyer. Everyone's situation is unique, and the lawyer will be able to determine what is best for you and can help walk you through the process. Be aware that filing for bankruptcy can negatively affect your credit history for up to ten years from the date of filing. Also, debts like student loans, child support, alimony, and unpaid taxes may not be expunged by filing for bankruptcy.

I Get Injured Without Health Insurance

Likelihood of Happening: Moderate
Ease of Prevention: High
Is Time a Factor? No

Despite the fact that health insurance coverage is now mandatory in the United States, tens of millions of Americans still lack even minimal coverage. For those living paycheck to paycheck, even a small medical issue like a broken bone or an overnight stay in a hospital can spell financial ruin.

■ Apply Immediately

The Affordable Care Act, which made health insurance coverage compulsory for all Americans, also contains a provision that prevents health insurance providers from denying coverage to individuals with pre-existing conditions. This includes everything from asthma, diabetes, cancer, and even chronic back pain and previous injuries. Unfortunately, you can only apply for coverage during the designated open enrollment period that usually begins sometime in October or November for plans starting on January 1 of the following year. There are some exceptions, though.

You can apply for coverage at any point during the year if you have recently experienced one of the following:

- Marriage or divorce
- Had or adopted a child, or placed a child up for adoption or in foster care
- Moved your residence, obtained citizenship, or were released from prison
- Lost health care coverage due to loss of employment, aging out of a parent's health care coverage, losing Medicaid or CHIP coverage, or a similar circumstance

So if the stars align, you might be able to apply for coverage immediately after the incident. Keep in mind, however, that your new coverage might not retroactively cover the expenses already incurred. It may only apply to future treatment.

■ Get Treated Anyway

While there are many small injuries that can be treated at home, failing to go to the hospital for others could cost you your life. Even if you do not have health insurance coverage, hospitals are required by law to provide you with the necessary treatment. If you are seriously injured, seek immediate medical treatment regardless of your financial status. Your life is far more important than the costs you will incur.

If your injury is relatively minor, you may be able to find a free clinic in your area that can provide sufficient care to handle the problem. While there may still be a small fee, it will likely be significantly less expensive than if you were to go to the emergency room. You may also be able to find a nonprofit group in your area that may be able to help you pay any bills you are unable to afford yourself.

■ Work with the Hospital

Once your injury has been successfully treated, you can sit down with an administrator at the hospital to discuss your options for paying for your care. In some cases, hospitals will reduce the amount owed dependent on your income, or set you up on a payment plan that will allow you to repay the debt over time. You may also be able to lower the debt if you agree to pay in cash. If you are uncomfortable handling the negotiations yourself, there are a variety of private companies that will handle the back and forth for you.

I Put a Hole Through My Wall

- **Likelihood of Happening:** Moderate
- **Ease of Prevention:** High
- **Is Time a Factor?** No

There are very few circumstances where it is acceptable to have a hole in your wall. These may or may not include a time when:

- You are installing a window
- You are in the process of knocking the wall down
- You are hiding political refugees in said wall
- You are in college

If you find yourself outside of the permissible boundaries, you are going to need to address the issue sooner or later—preferably sooner.

■ Decide If This Is Actually Your Problem

If you are the owner of the home, a hole in the wall is pretty much your problem. Even if you had nothing to do with the creation of this hole, it's yours now. Your only chance for a reprieve from the chore of fixing it is if a hired contractor like a plumber or electrician created the hole. But even then, the process for taking them to task might not be worth the trouble.

If you are a renter, however, the responsibility may fall on your land-lord, especially if you can prove the hole was there before you moved in. Even if you are solely at fault—perhaps you swatted a spider with a dumbbell instead of a newspaper, for example—your landlord may forbid you from making any repairs yourself. So check your lease carefully before you break out the spackle.

■ Patch It Up

Unless you want to hire a professional, you will need the following materials to get the job done:

- Spackle
- Putty knife
- Mesh patch
- Sponge
- Sandpaper
- Paint
- Paint roller

Before you start working, pick out any ragged pieces of drywall or plaster surrounding the hole. Next, sand all around the hole so you have a nice, even surface on which to apply the patch. Once it's sanded down, apply the patch directly over the hole so that it completely covers the hole, with room to spare.

Once the patch is securely in place—either using the self-adhesive backing of the patch or by spreading spackle around the edges— apply a generous amount of spackle around the sides of the patch as evenly as possible, leaving the middle uncovered for now. Wait approximately 20 minutes for it to dry, then cover the remaining portion of the patch. When the entirety of the patch is covered, allow it to dry overnight.

Technically your hole is no longer a hole at this point, but it probably doesn't look all that great, either. To neaten it up, use the sandpaper to gradually file down any excess spackle until the entire area is uniformly smooth. There will likely be a substantial amount of white particles that accumulate, so lay down some newspaper before sanding, or keep a broom or vacuum handy.

If your wall is precisely the same shade of white as the spackle, then congratulations, your job is done. In the extremely likely event that this isn't the case, you will need to track down the correct paint color and apply an even coating over any areas where white is showing through. While it may not be perfect—the color might be just a bit off, or there might be a few uneven spots—it's certainly a heck of a lot better than a gaping hole in your wall.

My Landlord Raises the Rent

- **Likelihood of Happening:** High
- **Ease of Prevention:** Low
- **Is Time a Factor?** No

Renting an apartment can be an expensive business. Naturally, you have to pay the first month's rent, and a security deposit makes perfect sense—the landlord is taking on some risk, after all. But then there's the last month's rent, which always feels more like a personal loan, and that real estate agent isn't going to show you around out of the goodness of her heart, so there's the broker fee to consider. So when it comes time to renew the lease, it's no wonder that most tenants lose their minds when they notice a rent increase.

■ Know Your Rights

The tenant/landlord relationship is a complicated one, and most states have special regulations in place to take some of the guesswork out of it. This includes provisions regarding when it's permissible to raise rent, as well as allowable percentage increases.

Before you do anything else, do some research and see if your landlord's proposed rent increase meets your state's guidelines. If, for example, it's only been a few months since you moved in, and your lease explicitly states the terms extend for a twelve-month period, then you might find your landlord is completely in the wrong.

■ Do the Math

Small increases in rent to keep up with inflation as well as the rising value of homes in the neighborhood should be expected. If the amount is reasonable, your best bet might be to suck it up and pay the increased rent. To determine what amount you are willing to pay, you will first need to weigh the increase against the cost of moving. If the increase is less, you should probably stay put. You should also shop around in your neighborhood to see the price of comparable rental units. This will help determine if moving is a wise investment, as well as provide leverage should you decide to negotiate with your landlord.

■ Talk to Your Landlord

Landlords are people, too, and hopefully yours is a reasonable one. If you feel the rent increase is unfair, or you simply can't afford to pay any more each month, then sit down with your landlord and discuss the matter. Good tenants are hard to come by, so it's quite possible you have some real bargaining power.

If your landlord won't budge on the increase, try negotiating other things as requirements for your renewal. An extra few hundred dollars a month should be more than enough to cover an in-unit washer and dryer or insulated windows, both of which would raise the value of the apartment as well as save you money.

There's always a chance you won't be able to come to any sort of agreement, and you'll be stuck either ponying up the extra cash or looking for a new place to call home. But hey, at least you tried.

There's Mold in My Bathroom

— **Likelihood of Happening:** Moderate
— **Ease of Prevention:** High
— **Is Time a Factor?** No

When you are in college, having a gross bathroom almost becomes a badge of honor rather than an embarrassment. "Look how busy I am! I don't even have time to wipe down the sink!"

As you get older, however, you take pride in maintaining a spotless bathroom bereft of soap scum, overflowing wastebaskets, and white toothpaste specks on the mirror. But even the cleanest of bathrooms can harbor a dark and dirty secret tucked away behind toilets or in the dark recesses of loose tiling: mold.

■ Choose Your Weapon

If you wait to take care of your mold problem it's only going to get worse, not better. In order to properly clean your bathroom you will need to start by emptying everything out, including shampoo bottles, toothbrushes, toilet paper, etc. Next, you'll need to choose a cleaning agent to deal with the mold. Options include:

- **Diluted Bleach:** A mixture of 1 part bleach to 10 parts of water should be enough to tackle any type of mold. The bleach may stain certain surfaces, so test it on a small, out-of-sight spot first.
- **Vinegar:** Applying undiluted vinegar directly to the mold will kill most mold species. While this option avoids the use of harsh chemicals, some find the odor to be offensive.
- **Off-the-Shelf Mold Cleaners:** Although significantly more expensive than most other options, they take the guesswork out of the equation and provide detailed instructions on their use.

Each method has its benefits and drawbacks, but any one of them should suffice to tackle your mold situation.

■ Get to Work

Once you've settled on your preferred cleanser, don a pair of gloves to protect your skin and a mask to avoid inhaling any spores. Apply the cleaner to any affected areas and allow it to stand for approximately fifteen minutes before scrubbing it vigorously with a sponge. Rinse the area and repeat the process if there are still visible signs of mold.

If the mold has penetrated your grout, you may want to replace it just to make sure you've gotten it all. If it's made its way behind your tiles, you may need to replace those as well, or even hire professional remediators to take care of the problem.

■ Keep Your Bathroom Mold Free

Once you've removed every speck of visible mold, your goal for the future is to keep it that way. A nice, moist bathroom is an ideal location for mold to take root, so you'll want to keep the exhaust fan running while you are showering, as well as after. If your bathroom has windows, be sure to open them periodically to allow fresh air to circulate. If your sink or bathtub drains slowly, they can become breeding grounds for mold growth; make sure you keep them free of any clogs. Cleaning your bathroom at least once a week will also go a long way toward preventing future mold outbreaks.

I Am Caught Speeding

Likelihood of Happening: High
Ease of Prevention: High
Is Time a Factor? No

For some, speed limits are more guidelines than hard and fast rules. Everyone knows you can drive a few miles per hour faster than the posted limit without getting pulled over—especially if you are late to work, you really have to use the bathroom, or you need to catch up with that guy who cut you off two miles back so you can give him the finger. Right, officer?

■ Be Polite and Respectful

Keep in mind that the officer didn't pull you over because he's a jerk or because he's bored. He pulled you over because you were speeding, and it's his job. So be polite.

Before the officer approaches your car, get your paperwork ready and lower all your windows—yes, all of them—to allow the officer a complete view of the interior of your car. The easier it is for the officer to evaluate any potential danger, the more at ease she will be. In addition, you want to keep your hands on the wheel unless otherwise instructed, to avoid creating unwanted tension.

■ Be Honest, but Don't Admit Guilt

This can be a little tricky, but you will want to walk the line between complying with the officer's request and incriminating yourself. When the officer asks, "Do you know why I pulled you over?" the safe and honest answer is "No, I don't." While you certainly might have an inkling, only the officer knows the answer to this question, and you should let her explain.

Don't offer any more information than is necessary to respectfully answer the officer's questions. Whenever possible, stick to "yes ma'am" and "no ma'am." Think carefully before you answer, as even seemingly innocuous statements like "I don't know how fast I was going" can come back to haunt you later—it implies you weren't paying attention to your speed.

■ Ask for a Warning

As long as you've been friendly, honest, and compliant up to this point, you've done all you can to tip the scales of avoiding a ticket in your favor. While you could leave it at that and cross your fingers, there's little harm in openly asking for a warning instead of a ticket.

This might require you to admit guilt and apologize for the infraction, but you could also leave it ambiguous and simply state you are sorry you forced the officer to get out of her vehicle. While there's no guarantee the officer will take pity on you, it's not likely to make your situation any worse.

■ Pay Your Fine or Have Your Day in Court

If you failed to convince the officer with your heartfelt plea for a warning, you will have to decide whether you want to simply pay the fine or battle the charges in court.

If you choose the latter option, start building your case immediately after the officer leaves the scene. For example, if there's a nearby speed limit sign that's been obstructed, take pictures to show in court. Pay close attention to the details of the ticket you've been issued and note any inaccuracies that might help you win your case.

Depending on the severity of the penalties, you might want to consider hiring a lawyer to help you with your case. He might have a better chance of having it dismissed, or at least negotiated down to an infraction with a less severe penalty.

I Get Into an Accident During a Test Drive

- **Likelihood of Happening:** Low
- **Ease of Prevention:** High
- **Is Time a Factor?** No

Test-driving a new car can be a lot of fun. You get to sit behind the wheel of a brand new model and push it to the limits of what you might encounter in your normal driving experience—and possibly a little beyond. Usually the experience goes smoothly and you bring the car back to the dealership minus a gallon of gas, but otherwise no worse for the wear. Usually . . .

■ Don't Be Blinded by Guilt

Regardless of whether or not the accident was your fault, you were the one behind the wheel when it happened. So naturally you feel at least somewhat responsible—and you very well may be. But that doesn't mean you should immediately break out your wallet and offer to pay for the damages.

Although it may feel like it, you are by no means the first person on earth to be involved in a traffic incident while test-driving a car. The dealership may have special insurance specifically devoted to this kind of situation, and it's quite possible you won't have to pay a dime.

■ Treat It Like Any Other Accident

There will be plenty of time to play the blame game later. For now, you want to attend to any injuries and start gathering information that might help you later. Assuming nobody is hurt, call the dealership and let them know that you've been in an accident. While you wait for them to send someone to help you deal with the situation, use the opportunity to take pictures of the scene and jot down notes of any important information about the accident that you might forget later. Call the police so they can send an officer down to assess the situation and allow you to file a formal report, which you may need later for insurance purposes.

The Safest Time to Drive

If you are nervous about getting into an accident while test-driving a fancy new car, reduce your risk by doing it in the early afternoon, avoiding the hours of 3:00 P.M. through 6:00 P.M., which is when most accidents occur. The second most dangerous time to drive is between 6:00 P.M. and midnight.

Figure Out Who Foots the Bill

The question of who has to pay for repairs is a tricky one, but in most cases responsibility falls to the owner of the vehicle. Luckily for you, the owner in this case is still the dealership, or the private seller if you responded to an ad online. While they may try to pressure you into filing a claim on your own insurance policy, it's quite likely they don't have a leg to stand on. If that happens, remain firm and consult a lawyer first before agreeing to take on any of the responsibility.

It's not uncommon, however, for dealerships to require customers to sign a waiver before they take a car for a test drive. Depending on the language of the document, you may have agreed to take partial or sole responsibility for any damages in the event of an accident. If you did sign such a waiver, your only option will be to file a claim under your own insurance. If you don't have insurance, you may find yourself responsible for the full cost of the vehicle out of pocket.

My Home Is Vandalized

- **Likelihood of Happening:** Moderate
- **Ease of Prevention:** Low
- **Is Time a Factor?** Yes

Your home may be your castle, but chances are slim you've gone to the same lengths as medieval lords did to protect it. Instead of a moat and a drawbridge, the only real deterrent most people bother with are motion-sensor lights and sturdy locks. Which might work to deter thieves, but they won't do much good if someone targets the exterior of your home rather than the valuables inside.

■ Don't Engage the Vandals

While there's a good chance you are merely dealing with a ragtag gang of adolescent hooligans, it's simply not worth the risk to try and scare them off your property on your own. Even passive attempts at retaliation like turning on your sprinkler system can escalate the situation and result in even more damage to your home.

If you catch the vandals in the act, call the police immediately and take note of the clothing and physical description of everyone involved. If you are able to do so without the vandals noticing, use your phone to take pictures or video of the carnage as it happens. This information will greatly increase the chance that the police will be able to apprehend them later. Before the police leave, ask to get a copy of the police report or a police report number for your records; however, you may need to go down to the station to obtain this information.

■ Document Everything

Once it's safe to do so, walk around your property with a camera and take pictures of every egg splatter, broken shingle, and stray piece of toilet paper on your property. Even if it's something that's relatively easy to clean up, like a smashed pumpkin on your driveway, you'll want to have evidence to show to your insurance company if you need to file a claim. You may also need to present this evidence to the police, should they track down the vandals.

After you've cataloged all the damage, call your home insurance company, as well as your automobile insurance provider if there is damage to your car. Even if you have pictures, they may need to send a claims adjuster to your home to verify the damage, so check with your insurance agent(s) before you start cleaning up.

■ Clean Up the Mess

When your home has been vandalized, you'll probably have a lot of cleanup to take care of once the police and your insurance agent have checked things out. Some common items that may be used to vandalize your home include eggs, shaving cream, toilet paper, and spray paint, which are certainly less dangerous than rocks and bricks, but can still be a chore to clean up. Make your job a little easier with the following tips:

- **Toilet Paper:** Obtain a few garbage bags and weigh them down with rocks to ensure they don't blow away. Gather up as much stray toilet paper as you can; use brooms or long sticks to remove any from your trees.

- **Eggs:** These are easiest to clean up before they have dried by spraying warm water from above to wash the splatter down the sides of your house. Just make sure to avoid hot water, as this could actually cook the egg and adhere it to the siding. Use a high-alkaline cleanser to remove any caked-on egg, as this will break down the fat and protein. For stains on your car, stick to warm water and dedicated car-washing detergent.

- **Shaving Cream:** A little laundry detergent and hot water should do the trick, both on your driveway and the walls of your home.

- **Spray Paint:** Some brands of spray paint can be removed with a simple mixture of warm water and liquid dish soap. If that doesn't do the trick, a nonacetone nail polish remover applied to a rag should make short work of it.

At the end of the day, take comfort in the fact that you've only lost a few hours of cleaning time during this whole ordeal—the vandals on the other hand may very well be jerks forever.

I Struck a Deer with My Car

- **Likelihood of Happening:** Moderate
- **Ease of Prevention:** Moderate
- **Is Time a Factor?** No

Depending on where you do the majority of your driving, you are either deathly afraid or blissfully unaware of the unpredictable ruminants grazing on the fringes of the highway. If you fall into the latter category, you will quickly migrate to the former the first time a deer materializes from out of nowhere and you smash into it at 65 mph. While it's quite the terrifying experience for the driver, imagine how it feels for the deer.

■ Embrace the Inevitable

When there's a 300-pound buck standing nonchalantly in the middle of your lane, you may only have a fraction of a second to react . . . which is almost never enough time to check your blind spot and safely veer your vehicle out of harm's way. If you do attempt to swerve, you run the risk of hitting another car or running off the road and striking a tree—both of which would be far worse than hitting a deer.

Instead, firmly apply the brakes, keep your hands steady on the wheel, and do your best to stay in your lane. If you are lucky, you will be able to come to a complete stop before you make contact with the animal. At the very least, you'll be able to slow down and minimize the damage caused by the impact.

■ Assess the Damage

Assuming your vehicle is still operable, pull off to the side of the road and turn on your hazard lights. Even if your car appears drivable, look closely for any leaking fluids or other indicators that it might be unsafe to move it.

Now it's time to see to the other victim of the accident. If the injured or deceased deer is in the middle of the highway, place road flares a safe distance from the animal to warn oncoming traffic. The deer may be frightened, so avoid getting too close. While it may be unsettling to stand idly by as you watch the animal suffer, attempting to aid the deer can put you at unnecessary risk. Although deer are generally harmless, it can use its powerful legs and sharp hooves to cause you serious injury if it feels threatened. The best course of action for both you and the deer is to alert the local authorities of the situation, so they can send trained professionals to assist.

■ Cut Your Losses

Venison may not be everyone's meal of choice, but if the deer didn't pull through and you're a fan of wild game, it would be a shame to let hundreds of pounds of deer meat go to waste. Before you start loading the carcass into your truck, however, be sure to alert the local authorities of the situation. Laws vary from state to state, but you could receive a hefty fine for not possessing the proper permit to keep the deer.

If you're not interested in the meat, many states have a call list in place for individuals who will happily come and take it off your hands.

Deer Aren't Stupid, Just Confused

Freezing in the middle of the road is a pretty poor defense mechanism when a 5,000-pound SUV is barreling toward you. The reason deer exhibit this behavior is because their pupils are fully dilated at night, and the sudden onslaught of light from the vehicle's headlights disorients them.

My House Is Robbed

- **Likelihood of Happening:** Moderate
- **Ease of Prevention:** Moderate
- **Is Time a Factor?** No

Nobody wakes up in the morning thinking their house will be robbed that day. Yet every year, millions of Americans come home from work to discover their home has been ransacked and all of their valuables have vanished without a trace. If you find yourself a victim of a burglary, what you do next can make all the difference when it comes to bringing the burglar to justice and maybe even recovering your stolen property.

■ Treat Your Home Like a Crime Scene . . . Because It Is

There may not be any caution tape blocking off your bedroom just yet, but for all intents and purposes you need to pretend that there is. It may be tempting to scour your home and take stock of what was taken and what the burglar missed, but right now your main priority is to call the police and leave everything just as it is. If you have any reason to suspect that the burglar may still be present in your home, immediately leave the premises and phone the authorities from a safe location.

While you wait for the police to arrive, walk around and take pictures of the aftermath. If anything was damaged, you will have a much easier time making an insurance claim if you have clear evidence that the damage occurred during the burglary—not after. This is especially effective if you also have pictures from before the burglary for comparison.

After the police arrive, they will ask you questions about when the robbery might have occurred and whether you've noticed any suspicious activity in the days leading up to the robbery. The more information you can give them, the better the chances that they will be able to track down the criminal.

■ Make a List and Check It Twice

Once the authorities have left, go through your home and write a detailed account of everything that is missing. Assuming the police have already investigated your home, it should be safe to move things around to make sure you haven't overlooked anything. This list should include absolutely *everything* that was stolen, from your big-screen TV to the pillowcases the thieves may have used to abscond with your smaller valuables.

With the list in hand, call your insurance company to begin the process of filing a claim. Your representative will likely ask you for your police report number, as well as additional information about the event. Be upfront and honest when answering your representative's questions, and be prepared to provide your list of what was stolen. Depending on your insurer as well as the value of what was stolen, a claims adjuster may need to visit your home to verify the authenticity of your claim.

■ Let the Police Handle the Detective Work

This should not come as a surprise, but watching crime dramas on television does not qualify you to be a detective. The police will do everything in their power to reclaim your stolen property, and they have far more experience with burglaries than you do.

If you must slip on your Sherlock Holmes deerstalker hat, keep your sleuthing to visiting local pawnshops and monitoring resale sites like Craigslist. If you do come across anything you believe could have once belonged to you, immediately forward the information to the police. Attempting to confront the seller yourself could be dangerous.

I Lose My Cell Phone

- **Likelihood of Happening:** High
- **Ease of Prevention:** High
- **Is Time a Factor?** Yes

These days our cell phones are more than just miniature computers we carry in our pockets; they are our lives. Sure, we use them to make calls and send text messages, but they also serve as music players, task managers, alarm clocks, calendars, financial advisors, entertainment centers, GPS navigators, flashlights, and countless other things. They even capture and store our family photos—as well as our more private ones. So it's safe to say that losing one is more than just a minor inconvenience.

■ Send Out an SOS Beacon

Unlike a wallet or most other lost objects, your smartphone is one of the few things you can still communicate with once it's misplaced.

Before you go scrambling around to find it, borrow a phone from a friend—or track down one of the last few remaining pay phones on earth—and dial your number. With any luck, someone close to it will hear the ringing, pick it up, and you can organize a way to pick it up.

You can also send a text message with your first name and an e-mail address or alternate phone number for someone to reach you, should they find the phone later. With many modern smartphones, text messages will appear on the screen even if the phone is locked.

■ Check Your Software

Because you are not the first smartphone user to ever misplace one, manufacturers have been developing ways to reunite customers with their phones for years. Most phones come with preinstalled software that will allow you to sign into your account and discover its precise location. This can save you hours of frantic searching and retracing your steps.

The only drawback is that your phone needs to be powered on in order for this feature to work. If your battery dies, or somebody scooped it up and turned it off, then you are out of luck.

■ Lock It Down

Considering all of the sensitive information contained on a modern smartphone, this is actually one case where it's wise to be overly cautious. If your phone isn't password protected, any unsavory individual who picks it up instantly gains access to your e-mail, social media, and possibly even your banking information.

Depending on the phone you have—or had—the same software that can help you pinpoint its location also allows you to lock it remotely. If you know for a fact it was stolen and there's no hope of recovering it, you may even be able to render it completely unusable this way.

While you may feel it's overkill, you would also be wise to change all of your passwords for any apps and services you use on your smartphone. This includes banks, e-mail, social media, and even things like online dating apps . . . really, anything someone could use to impersonate you and steal your identity. Although it's unlikely that someone who finds your phone will be interested in doing anything but selling it, it's always better to be safe than sorry.

I Lose My Wallet

Likelihood of Happening: High
Ease of Prevention: High
Is Time a Factor? Yes

As we continue to rely more heavily on technology, the importance we place on the almighty wallet is dwindling. According to a report by Bankrate.com, around half of Americans carry less than twenty dollars in cash with them each day. Gone are the days when doting fathers kept dozens of portraits of their children tucked away behind their AAA cards. But even though we may be placing less value on the old standby, it can still be a devastating blow if it should happen to go missing.

■ Rule Out Places It Isn't

The old adage "it's always in the last place you look" is certainly accurate, but that's simply because nobody keeps searching for a missing item once it's been found. Absent from that archaic sentiment is all that time that could have been saved by not looking in all the wrong places.

By thinking back to the last place you remember having your wallet, you can immediately rule out all the locations you traveled to before that time. There's no point in running back to the gym if you know you purchased a latte at Starbucks right after yoga.

Once you've determined where it's not, try to track down where it is. Call every restaurant, retail store, and other location you've been in since you last used your wallet and see if someone has handed it in. Even if you come up short, leave your name and contact information in case it turns up later.

■ Catalog Everything in Your Wallet

Once your wallet goes missing, sit down and make a list of everything contained in your wallet. Yes, this can be exceptionally difficult when your wallet isn't right in front of you, but you should still be able to make a fairly comprehensive list from memory.

Your driver's license, credit cards, and store loyalty cards should be easy to recall, but don't forget things like museum passes, library cards, and gym memberships. Ordering replacements now will save you from having to deal with it at the last minute when you actually need to use them.

■ Hope for the Best, but Assume the Worst

While there's always a chance a Good Samaritan will come through for you, if you can't track your wallet down by backtracking it's best to assume your wallet is never coming back. And if it's in the hands of an especially dishonest passerby—or even a professional thief—the longer you wait to accept that fact, the worse off you'll be.

Along with the cash you had folded inside, your wallet could easily contain thousands of dollars of potential risk in the form of credit and debit cards. So grab your list of what was in your wallet, because the sooner you get on the phone to place holds on your cards, the easier it will be for you to dispute any fraudulent charges later. This is especially important for debit cards, because unlike credit cards, the responsibility for any charges falls squarely on you should you fail to report the card as lost or stolen.

While it may seem futile, you should also call the police and file an official report. At the very least, this will help you if you need to reverse any charges later.

People Are Not As Honest As They Claim

Although nearly 60 percent of people insist they would try to track down the owner of a wallet or hand it in to police, only one in five actually do so. When researchers in England dropped twenty wallets and purses in each of five major cities, only 20 percent were recovered. Of those, only 55 percent still contained the original amount of cash contained within them.

A Tree Falls on My House

Likelihood of Happening: Low
Ease of Prevention: Low
Is Time a Factor? No

Trees have a lot to offer the humble homeowner. They offer shade, a location for a quaint swing or hammock, and fresh fruit. When combined with other tasteful landscaping, they can even raise your property value as much as 20 percent. But as the saying goes, "the bigger they are, the harder they fall," which is especially problematic when they happen to come down on your roof.

■ Think of Your Family Before Your Home

A fully mature oak tree can grow to a height of more than 100 feet and weigh in at more than 14 tons. The damage this can cause to a home is sizable, but the greater concern is what an object of this size could do to a human being. Before you begin to evaluate the state of your house, make sure that everyone residing in the home is present and accounted for. If anyone is injured or trapped by debris, immediately call 911 for assistance.

Even if everyone appears unharmed, the damage could have compromised the structural integrity of your home. The safest course of action is to immediately vacate the premises, especially if there are any downed wires.

■ Assess the Damage

Removing your bulky new houseguest and repairing the damage will be an expensive undertaking, but this is why you have homeowner's insurance. When filing your claim, it will be helpful to have documentation of all the damage caused by the falling tree. From a safe distance, take tons of pictures and video of all of the areas of your home that were affected. Also be sure to capture footage of any damage to your neighbor's property—or lack thereof. You will want to be extremely thorough here, and document any damage caused to other landscaping, cars parked in the driveway, and any personal belongings found on your property. While it's true that your policy may not cover everything, it's better to have too much evidence than not enough.

The World's Largest Single Tree

Nobody wants to deal with a massive maple tree in their dining room, but you can at least take comfort in the fact that it could have been worse. The world's largest tree, a giant sequoia known as General Sherman, stands at 275 feet tall with a diameter of 25 feet.

■ Work with Your Insurance Company

You may not have a clue how to go about removing a 28,000-pound log from your property, but your insurance company knows someone who does. They will also have a list of contractors to help you with everything from roof repair to replacing your water fountain that's now in 1,000 pieces. Most importantly, they will be able to assist you with temporary housing while the folks you hire to clean up the mess make your home livable again.

My House Is Flooded

- **Likelihood of Happening:** Moderate
- **Ease of Prevention:** Low
- **Is Time a Factor?** Yes

We often forget how devastating the forces of nature can be until they come knocking on our front door—quite literally in some cases. Whether an unexpected deluge descends on your home, or a burst water main turns your living room into a swimming pool, nobody wants to be waist deep in water with no idea what to do next.

■ Be Smart and Safe, not Stupid and Dead

Before you start scrambling to pluck any valuables from the depths, be mindful of the fact that water and electricity do not go very well together. If you can't reach the main breaker from a safe, dry spot, do not under any circumstances attempt to switch it off. Instead, call the fire department.

Once you are certain there isn't a danger of electrocution, your next task is to listen and smell for leaking gas. If you believe there may be a leak—caused by damage from floating debris or pressure on the gas lines—immediately open a window, vacate the premises, and shut off the main valve outside your home.

Lastly, before you begin moving around in the muck and mire, don waterproof boots and gloves to protect yourself from any harmful bacteria that could be lurking in the water. During floods, it's quite common for sewage lines to back up and mix with the floodwater.

■ Document Everything

While it's perfectly clear to you now that there's a flood in your home—you are standing in several feet of water, after all—you will eventually need to prove all of this to your insurance company. If your camera or cell phone hasn't been lost in the flood, take this opportunity to capture photos of anything and everything you think may have been damaged by the water. It may be tempting to try to salvage some of your personal items, but there will be plenty of time for that after you have a record of all of the damage, and you've dealt with the water.

■ Break Out the Wet Vac

If you have several feet of water in your home, it's time to call in the professionals. If you only have a few inches to deal with, however, you should be able to remove it yourself with a wet vac—a vacuum specifically designed to handle liquid spills. But be forewarned, this may take a while.

After you've removed the bulk of the water—several painstaking gallons at a time—close all the windows and set up a network of fans and a dehumidifier to eliminate excess moisture in the air and help dry out your carpeting, if you have any. If the water has been sitting for some time, your best bet will be to dispose of the carpeting entirely, but if you work fast you may be able to salvage it.

■ Disinfect Your Home

Congratulations, the water is gone and your house is starting to look relatively normal again. Your next step is to disinfect the heck out of every surface that came into contact with water. The U.S. Department of Public Health recommends a mixture of bleach and water to get the job done and ensure you kill any bacteria or mold that might have started growing on your walls and floors. Dry wall and insulation are very difficult to dry and disinfect, and you are better off removing them than attempting to salvage them.

As for personal belongings, you will likely be able to save some by cleaning them with the same diluted bleach solution, but others you will need to part with. Things like waterlogged mattresses, books, upholstered furniture, and stuffed animals can be very dangerous to keep, as they are difficult to dry and disinfect thoroughly. Any nonporous items, however, should be salvageable.

You Can't Stop a Flood, but You Can Outthink It

If you happen to live in an area prone to flooding, there are a few steps you can take to protect your home:

- Fortify your entryways with sandbags to prevent floodwater from entering your home.
- Move all expensive and porous items as high up as you can.
- Place small valuables and irreplaceable sentimental objects in sealed plastic bags and place them on the top level of your home on top of furniture or hung from the ceiling.
- Firmly shut all doors and windows prior to a storm, and don't open them until water levels recede.

I Drop My Wedding Ring Down the Drain

- **Likelihood of Happening:** Moderate
- **Ease of Prevention:** High
- **Is Time a Factor?** No

Based on anecdotal evidence, wedding rings have a natural affinity for drainage pipes. Even if you leave it inside a locked jewelry box in the bedroom, your ring will, somehow, magically teleport to the edge of the kitchen sink while you are doing dishes. It is known. What many people don't realize is that your sink doesn't lead directly to the ocean, and chances are quite high that you can retrieve your wayward trinket.

■ Think It Through

The first thing you should do is turn off the water and step back from the sink. Take a moment to curse yourself and sulk. Embrace the fact that no matter how hard you will it to, your ring is not going to spontaneously shoot back out of the drain. If you want to get it back, you are going to have to roll up your sleeves and get your hands dirty.

Now, the anatomy of kitchen plumbing is as foreign as the dark side of the moon to many homeowners, but retrieving your ring is on the short list of things you don't need to call a plumber for. This is because it is almost certainly lodged in the P-trap (a.k.a. the U-bend), the U-shaped portion of pipe under your sink. It's designed to prevent backflow, but also offers the fringe benefit of trapping foreign objects that make their way down the drain.

■ Get Ready to Get Messy

If you are like most people who have never mucked around with plumbing, the space underneath your sink is probably filled with an array of cleaning supplies and other odds and ends. Clear all that out and replace it with an empty bucket to catch any leakage.

(Caution: You may want to hold your nose before attempting this next portion.)

Next, loosen the two threaded caps—these should loosely resemble the screw cap for a soda bottle—at both ends of the P-trap and remove the portion of pipe. If your sink was slightly clogged before you started this whole process, prepare for a small deluge of water, hair, food particles, a multitude of other smelly, unpleasant debris, and—hopefully—your precious ring.

At this point, feel free to perform a little victory dance or give thanks to the deity of your choosing. Before reconnecting the P-trap, take a moment to clean it with a stiff brush to dislodge any additional gunk that may have built up over time. Once it's back in place, run the faucet for a few seconds and check for any leaks. If everything is flowing normally, you can tidy up and place your ring securely back on your finger where it belongs. If everything is not flowing normally, the good news is you have your ring back—the bad news is you need to call a plumber.

My Identity Is Stolen

- **Likelihood of Happening:** Moderate
- **Ease of Prevention:** High
- **Is Time a Factor?** Yes

There was a time when social security numbers and banking information were safely guarded information. If a thief wanted to empty your checking account, he had to physically travel to a bank—stolen account details in hand—and convince the teller that he was actually you. But nowadays, all he needs is access to your e-mail, Facebook account, or even just your garbage.

■ Understand What's at Risk

Identify theft is an incredibly broad term that can take a number of different forms, which most commonly include:

- Using stolen credit card details to purchase goods
- Opening lines of credit in your name
- Moving funds from your checking/savings accounts
- Posing as you to scam your friends and family

The danger of identity theft in the technology age is that a thief can focus on any combination of these forms—or even all of them simultaneously. For example, if your e-mail account is compromised, a thief now has a record of which banks you use, and can use that information to reset your passwords and gain access. He can change the address of your credit cards and have new ones sent to him instead of you. If you use the same password for your e-mail that you do for social media—which many people do—he can contact your friends and family and scam them into sending him money. Basically, once one of your accounts has been compromised, the best course of action is to assume that all of them have.

■ Act Fast and Think Broad

The first inkling that your identity is at risk may be easy to overlook. Perhaps you get a password reset notification from your bank that you didn't initialize, or your friend notices you were signed into Facebook at a time when you are certain you weren't. Instead of brushing it off, you need to act—and quickly.

First and foremost, contact one of the three credit reporting agencies (TransUnion, Equifax, or Experian) and place a fraud alert on your credit report. Doing so is free, and it will also enable you to obtain a free copy of your credit report from each agency—a benefit that is usually only available once annually—to analyze for inconsistencies.

Next, start calling contact numbers for each of the accounts affected to place holds on credit cards and temporarily lock down your bank funds. For online accounts, immediately log in and change all of your passwords. Since you don't know the extent of the information the thief has at his disposal, it's best to overreact here. While you might not think a thief could break into your PayPal account with information gleaned from your e-mail, it's better to be safe than sorry.

■ Alert the Authorities and Your Friends

The sooner you get the authorities involved, the better. You should be able to file a police report over the phone and obtain a report number. This will then allow you to file an Identity Theft Affidavit with the Federal Trade Commission and create an Identity Theft Report. This step is imperative if you need to reverse any unauthorized transactions on your credit card or from your bank accounts, or close any new accounts opened in your name.

When it comes to alerting your friends and family, social media is a powerful tool that you should absolutely employ. Once you've changed all your passwords, in just a matter of minutes you can e-mail everyone in your address book and post messages on your various accounts to remove the thief's ability to scam your social network. Fear of embarrassment can lead many to avoid this crucial step, but you need to remember that being a victim of identity theft is nothing to be ashamed of. The only one at fault here is the thief.

I Lose My Job

- **Likelihood of Happening:** Moderate
- **Ease of Prevention:** Low
- **Is Time a Factor?** No

According to a recent poll conducted by the *Washington Post*, more than 60 percent of Americans are worried about losing their jobs, which is justifiable in an age when unemployment rates sit above 6 percent. Yet even with the possibility of layoffs hanging over everyone's heads, very few workers actually have a plan in place for what to do if they find themselves unemployed.

■ File for Unemployment

This may sound like a no-brainer, but some studies indicate that more than a third of those eligible for unemployment benefits don't apply for them. This could be due to a number of factors including pride, optimism concerning length of unemployment, ignorance of eligibility, or confusion when applying. But at the end of the day, there is no legitimate excuse for not taking advantage of unemployment benefits. If you lost your job due to no fault of your own, the worst that can happen if you apply is you discover you are not eligible.

■ Square Away Health Insurance

Health insurance is expensive, but falling ill without coverage is a whole lot worse. Something as common as resetting a broken bone can cost upwards of $10,000 without insurance—a devastating blow to someone relying solely on unemployment benefits. While it can be tempting to forgo coverage until you secure new employment, this simply is not the area to cut costs. If you are married, you may have the option to move to your spouse's plan. Otherwise, you can apply for COBRA coverage through your previous health insurance provider or seek individual health care insurance options either through private insurance options or via the government-sponsored plans available under the Affordable Health Care Act.

■ Cut Your Spending

While you may not need to switch to a ramen noodle diet yet, cutting out any unnecessary spending will help increase the time you have until you get to that point.

If you eat out a lot, it's time to head to the grocery store and start cooking at home. Eliminate all the areas where you pay others to do things you could easily do yourself (like washing your car or housecleaning). When it comes to entertainment, you don't want to completely remove all leisure from your budget, as you'll need to keep your spirits up while you search for new jobs. Instead, think of ways you can trim down, like renting movies instead of going to the theater, or watching sporting events with friends instead of paying for an expensive cable package.

If you do not already maintain a budget plan for yourself, now would be a good time to draft up a detailed list of expenditures and allocate funds to various areas. You can use a simple spreadsheet or utilize one of several websites that will monitor your spending and help you adjust your budget accordingly.

■ Find a New Job

If there's one thing you have on your side now that you are unemployed, it's time. Approximately forty hours a week to be exact. Before you fill that time with housework and soap operas, embrace the idea that finding a job is your new nine-to-five.

Devote a fair amount of time and effort into updating your resume, and consider having it professionally designed and edited. Audit all of your social media accounts and ensure there's nothing that might concern a potential employer. At the same time, rework any career-centered accounts you might maintain to ensure you are putting your best face forward.

Next, pull out all the stops when it comes to networking. Get in touch with former colleagues and friends who work in your industry to see if they can help you acquire any leads. While you do that, research companies you would like to work for and closely monitor their individual career pages, as well as broader job boards specific to your field.

Unfortunately, finding a job is not something you can bull your way through with brute force. Even if you do devote forty hours a week to the search, you might still be out of work for many months. But the important thing is to remain upbeat and confident that you will eventually find a job.

I Start a Grease Fire

- **Likelihood of Happening:** Moderate
- **Ease of Prevention:** High
- **Is Time a Factor?** Yes

When you are heating oil in a pan to fry up some fish fillets, the possibility that it could spontaneously burst into flames probably isn't high on the list of things you're thinking about. But if you leave the pan unattended for too long, you could be greeted with a flaming, smoky kitchen when you come back.

■ Leave the Water in the Sink

When people encounter a small, contained fire, one instinctive reaction is to dump a glass of water on it in the hopes of smothering it. And oftentimes that approach works just fine—but not with grease fires. If you've ever dropped even a small amount of water into a pan of hot oil, you'll notice that this causes the oil to sputter. The same is true when the oil is on fire, except the sputter will become a rising fireball instead of a blip of jumping oil.

■ Smother the Flames

Fires need three things to continue burning:

1. Heat
2. Oxygen
3. Combustible material

There's not much you can do about the third element, but you can certainly address the first two. If it's safe to do so, turn off the burner on the stove. Next, outfit yourself with oven mitts and carefully place a metal lid or cookie sheet over the pan to cut off the oxygen supply. Avoid using glass lids or baking dishes, as the extreme heat of the flame can cause them to shatter. If this doesn't work, and the fire is relatively small, pouring a box of baking soda into the pan could be enough to smother it.

■ Grab the Right Fire Extinguisher

Fire extinguishers come in many shapes and sizes, and some can actually do more harm than good when it comes to a grease fire. While not very popular, a water-based extinguisher—Class A—would be a disaster. Instead, grab a Class B or Class K extinguisher and be sure to stand a fair distance away from the flames before you use it. If you stand too close, you risk propelling the oil—and flames—throughout your kitchen and spreading the fire instead of putting it out. Be forewarned, however, that discharging an extinguisher in your kitchen could result in chemical contamination. That said, it's far better to have a contaminated kitchen than a burned down house.

The Don'ts of Kitchen Fires

In the case of grease fires, knowing what *not* to do is just as important as knowing how to put the fire out. Aside from dousing the fire with water, you should also avoid:

- Carrying the pot outside to protect your home
- Using flammable materials to smother the fire
- Swatting at the flames
- Pouring anything other than baking soda over the flames

My Bike Is Stolen

Likelihood of Happening: Moderate
Ease of Prevention: High
Is Time a Factor? No

Bike theft is a booming industry, with some surveys indicating that more than 50 percent of all cyclists have had their ride stolen at some point. What's more concerning is the disturbingly low number of stolen bikes that are ever recovered: an abysmal 2.4 percent. While those figures may seem daunting, there are steps you can take to help you beat the odds.

■ Don't Give Up Hope

Many bike thefts go unreported, because victims simply shrugged, walked home, and washed their hands of the whole situation. While it may seem like an exercise in futility, your first step should be to call the police to report the bike stolen. Even if they never recover your bike, you may need to prove you filed a report in order to make an insurance claim. If you witnessed the bike being stolen—or someone nearby did—provide a description of the thief to give police something to work with.

■ Scour the Physical and Digital World

Chances are pretty good that whoever stole your bike isn't interested in riding it around. He's interested in selling it. This works heavily in your favor, as far as recovery goes.

Bike thieves don't often travel great distances to rip off cyclists; they stay close to home, which means that it's quite likely your bike isn't that far from where you lost it. Travel around your neighborhood and keep your eyes peeled. If you do happen to come across a bike that resembles the one that was stolen from you, check the serial number to verify that it is actually yours.

You should also call up local bike shops to alert them of the theft and ask them to keep an eye out for anyone bringing in your ride for repairs or seeking to sell it outright. If your bike has any unique characteristics—for example, stickers or noticeable marks—be sure to let them know when you call. You can also put up posters to get members of the community working on your side to track down your bike.

In today's day and age, you may even be able to track down your bike online. Sites like Craigslist are a smorgasbord of stolen goods, and chances are fairly good your thief will post your ride somewhere.

■ Set Up a Sting

If you are lucky enough to find your bike out in the wild or posted on the Internet, resist the urge to confront the thief yourself. Doing so puts you in danger, and you could also fail to apprehend the thief and miss out on your one opportunity to recover your stolen bike.

Instead, alert the authorities of the posting and work with them to contact the thief posing as a potential buyer. If all goes according to plan, you'll not only retrieve your precious transportation, but you'll also potentially prevent other cyclists from sharing a similar fate in the future.

I Get My Smartphone Wet

- **Likelihood of Happening:** Moderate
- **Ease of Prevention:** High
- **Is Time a Factor?** Yes

Despite the large sums of money we shell out for the privilege of carrying miniature computers in our pockets, we take shockingly poor care of our cell phones. We drop them incessantly, yet we can't be bothered to cover them with a proper case. We know there's no cell service in the middle of the ocean but we absolutely refuse to leave them back on shore. And God forbid we leave our precious smartphone in the other room while we use the toilet. While cracked screens, scuffed backs, or occasional dings and dents are little more than a nuisance, a short dip in a puddle on the street can be a death sentence for your phone if you don't act quickly.

■ Try Silica Gel

After you are done with your stream of expletives, calmly reach down into the sink, toilet, bowl of soup, or other container of liquid and retrieve your soggy cell phone. If your phone is still on, power it down immediately to prevent it from short-circuiting. If it is already off, do not under any circumstances attempt to turn it on. Instead, gently wipe it with a towel and put it aside while you consider the following question:

"How capable am I of taking a phone apart and putting it back together?"

If your answer is, "Wait, you can do that?" track down some silica gel—which you can find at pet stores masquerading as crystal-style cat litter—and submerge your phone in the bag. The gel acts as a moisture-wicking agent and is far superior to rice, couscous, or other alternatives. If your phone has a removable battery, take that out first and place it in the bag separately. Also be sure to remove your headphones from the headphone jack if you haven't already.

After five or so days, it's time to say a short prayer and attempt to turn it back on. If you find yourself staring at a blank screen, you may have to bite the bullet and take it apart.

■ Crack Open Your Phone

First and foremost, it's important to be aware that opening a cell phone can sometimes void the warranty. However, the chances are quite good that the warranty was already voided the moment your phone decided to take a swim around the bottom of a lake. That said, if your phone is currently just a fancy paperweight, what do you have to lose by taking it apart?

The methodology for opening your smartphone varies drastically from phone to phone, but there are a few consistencies regardless of the manufacturer. Once you remove the phone's backing and have gained access to the internals, you should be able to blast out any accumulated water droplets using a can of compressed air. It's unlikely you will need to completely disassemble the phone in order to do this. Instead, you only want to break it down to a point where all of the internals are exposed.

While you could reassemble your phone now and attempt to turn it on, the far safer approach is to let the disassembled components air dry—or ideally pack them in a bowl of silica gel—for a few days first. This final step should ensure that any stray moisture you might have missed has ample time to evaporate.

■ Practice Prevention

If you've managed to resurrect your phone, you've been given a second chance—so don't blow it. If you absolutely must have your phone with you at all times, consider investing in a waterproof case or storing it in a waterproof bag during situations where it is likely to get wet (like kayaking, paddle boarding, or lounging by the pool).

CHAPTER 4

Obnoxious Hassles and General Pains in the A**

It's unlikely your ideal Sunday consists of searching for your lost dog for seven hours or rescuing your car from a frosty tomb of snow. Unfortunately, not wanting to deal with these issues isn't going to make life's little annoyances disappear. While you'd rather be doing anything but addressing any of these major inconveniences, at least you'll know how to handle them should you be forced to.

I Can't Sleep

- **Likelihood of Happening:** High
- **Ease of Prevention:** Moderate
- **Is Time a Factor?** No

Some people possess a superhuman power that allows them to fall asleep at a moment's notice. They could be in the middle of a rock concert and nod off as if their folding metal chair were a comfortable pillow top mattress. For the rest of the world, sleep comes a little less easily—and sometimes not at all.

■ Don't Obsess

An inability to fall asleep is often a self-perpetuating problem. When you have trouble sleeping, you often fixate on how tired you are going to be in the morning and focus all of your attention on getting to sleep. Because you are so focused on the task at hand, you are unable to relax and get to sleep.

Like many things, sleep comes most readily when you aren't actively looking for it. Instead of focusing on the end goal of falling asleep, turn your attention to merely relaxing your body and breathing slowly and evenly. Sometimes merely stretching your muscles to relieve tension is enough to help you relax and get some rest.

■ Change Up Your Bedroom

The ideal sleeping space is dark, warm, comfortable, and free of erratic, unpredictable sounds. If light streams in from outside, draw the curtains or hang blankets over the windows. If you find that you wake up because you are cold, crank up the heat or invest in an electric blanket to keep your body temperature up through the night. If your mattress is too soft, place plywood underneath to firm it up. If it's too hard, rotate it around, place soft blankets on top of it, or consider investing in a pillowtop mattress pad. If you find you are frequently woken up by sudden noises, turn on a fan to drown out the sounds or consider purchasing a white noise maker. Some people also have success with quiet, soothing music.

■ Trick Your Brain

We may be the most intelligent species on the planet, but not even humans are immune to a little mental manipulation. For example, researchers have found that subjects who keep their eyes wide open and repeat the phrase "I will not sleep" often fall asleep more quickly than those who actively try to sleep. While they are uncertain what causes this paradoxical outcome, many believe it is due to the brain's poor ability to process negative statements.

You also might be able to trigger sleep by mimicking body movements that normally accompany sleep, such as rolling your eyes upwards into your head or relaxing your muscles one by one, moving from your toes to your head.

There are times when an inability to get to sleep is indicative of a serious disorder instead of just a stressful evening. If you experience long periods of sleeplessness, consider consulting a doctor to rule out any serious medical conditions.

My Car Is Encased in Snow and Ice

Likelihood of Happening: Moderate
Ease of Prevention: Moderate
Is Time a Factor? No

If you live in an area that gets hit with a lot of snow each winter, you are probably well aware of the importance of digging your car out immediately following a snowstorm, before the snow hardens. If you let it sit too long, you risk turning a relatively painless chore into something resembling an archaeological excavation.

■ Use the Right Tools for the Job

Clearing the snow away from your snow-encased car may not be rocket science, but it's going to be a lot more difficult if all you have to work with are your hands and a five-dollar ice scraper you got at a gas station. To do the job easily and efficiently, you will need:

- Shovel
- Soft-bristled broom
- Ice scraper
- Waterproof gloves
- Warm waterproof coat

While not necessary, you could also benefit from:

- Foam brush—a padded tool resembling a squeegee
- Wheelbarrow

Once you have everything assembled, it's time to brave the elements and rescue your car from its icy prison.

■ Look at the Big Picture

While it is easy to become overwhelmed with the enormity of the task at hand, try to think of the snow as a massive block of marble and the entombed car within as the finished sculpture. With that in mind, your first task is to start scraping away large chunks of snow to get closer to something resembling an automobile.

First, don your winter attire and shovel out a path to give yourself room to walk around the entirety of your car. If your town has laws prohibiting you from tossing snow into the street, having a wheelbarrow handy into which to dump the snow will make this portion much easier. If not, be prepared to make a lot of trips to your backyard. If the snow is particularly high, you will also want to shovel out the areas surrounding your doors to make sure you can open them all comfortably.

■ Clear Off the Car

When it comes to clearing off the actual car, start with the roof and use your broom to sweep as much snow as possible off to the side. If you are particularly concerned about scratching the paint, you can use a towel or foam brush for this task instead. Once the majority of the snow is gone from the roof, remove the snow from the hood and trunk of your car as well.

Next, use your broom to remove any snow from the front and back windshield, and all of the windows. Then break out the ice scraper to clear away any ice that may have accumulated. If the tailpipe is clear of snow, you can also turn on the car's engine and run the defroster for a while to make this task easier. Clearing snow and debris from the tailpipe is crucial, as failing to do so could put you at risk for carbon monoxide poisoning.

If there is a thin layer of ice anywhere else on your car, using the scraper could scratch the paint. Instead, strike the ice with your hand several times and then brush it off. If it's on the hood and it doesn't crack, the heat from the engine should gradually start to melt the ice.

Don't agonize over every last speck of ice and snow. As long as the majority of your car is clear, and there's no risk of large clumps of snow flying off your car to obstruct other motorists, you are free to drive to your destination.

My Car Battery Died

- **Likelihood of Happening:** High
- **Ease of Prevention:** High
- **Is Time a Factor?** No

Every day for years, you've hopped into your car and gone about your day without a hitch. You've run errands, dropped your kids off at daycare, and gone on road trips with your friends. But as with all good luck streaks, your record for consecutive days without a dead car battery has to eventually come to an end.

■ Crack Open the Hood

Before you start poking around in the innards of your car, take a moment to make sure that your battery is actually causing the problem. If your engine turns over but your car won't start, or if your radio, headlights, and all the other electronics in your car are devoid of life, chances are pretty good your battery is dead as a doornail.

Once you're sure that your battery is the problem, you need to determine if the battery is salvageable. Open the hood and inspect the exterior of the battery for cracks or any leaking fluids. If you see either, call a professional for assistance.

■ Jump-Start Your Car

Assuming the battery is still in good shape, you might be able to coax it back to life by jump-starting it. If you happen to have a jump-starting unit that plugs into your car's cigarette lighter, simply follow the instructions for your particular model and your car should be back up and running in no time.

If all you have is a set of jumper cables—or nothing—then you are going to need to get some help. You might get lucky and attract the attention of a Good Samaritan, but barring that you will need to call a friend or relative with a car to come bail you out. Bonus points if they have jumper cables and know how to use them.

When your friend arrives, have her park her functioning automobile front-to-front with your disabled one and turn her ignition off. Pop open both hoods, break out the jumper cables, and locate the batteries in both cars. Before you attach the cables, take note of the positive and negative terminals of the batteries, which should be marked with a plus sign and a negative sign respectively. Attach one positive cable to the positive terminal in the dead battery, and the other to the positive terminal of the functioning battery. Now, attach a negative cable to the negative terminal of the functioning battery. Instead of doing the same for the dead battery, attach the last cable to a secure metal component of the disabled car, such as a nut or bolt.

Turn on the functioning car and let it run for around ten minutes to give the dead battery time to charge. Then attempt to start the disabled car and, if the ignition turns over, allow it to run for a few more minutes with all the cables still attached. Carefully remove the cables in the opposite order in which you attached them. You will want to drive your car or let it idle for an additional twenty minutes or so, but if it's made it this far then chances are pretty good your battery will live to fight another day.

My Neighbor Won't Return Something

- **Likelihood of Happening:** High
- **Ease of Prevention:** High
- **Is Time a Factor?** No

Some things we'll happily lend to a neighbor without any hope of seeing them again. A cup of sugar, some mulch, that hideous pink flamingo you bought in 1997. But that $500 snow blower? You're going to want that one back. While most neighbors will readily return what is rightfully yours, there's always the chance you'll instead be met with "What snow blower?"

■ Audit the Value of Your Stuff

Before you start banging down doors, sit down and take stock of the value of the wayward item weighed against the potential fallout of demanding it back. Unlike a deadbeat friend who you can usually avoid when things go south, a neighbor is going to be a constant fixture until one of you moves.

There isn't a magic number when it comes to writing off your borrowed possessions, so you will have to determine how important it is to get your stuff back. If it's helpful, create a pros and cons list to help you decide how to proceed.

◼ Bring It Up Casually

Some people are just forgetful, and it's possible you are mistaking ignorance for malice. The next time you see your neighbor, casually insert the matter into the conversation. There's a good chance you'll receive your missing item along with a swift apology in short order.

If your neighbor still doesn't get the hint, you may need to be a bit more direct. Keep the discussion light, but make it clear that you need the item returned soon. Your neighbor may request to hang on to it for just a little longer, in which case you can decide for yourself whether he legitimately needs it or if this is just a stalling tactic.

> ### There's an App for That
> There are several apps and services that let users keep track of items they lend to friends and neighbors. An app called You Borrowed It allows you to upload photos of the item, so there's no disputing later who is the rightful owner.

◼ Move from Passive Aggression to Active Aggression

You both know damn well that the orange power drill is yours—it has your initials on the handle, for Pete's sake. So there's no sense in beating around the bush anymore. If your repeated reminders and polite requests continue to go unheeded, take the bull by the horns and firmly demand your stuff back.

Approach your neighbor and inform him that you simply can't wait any longer and you need the item returned immediately. Don't make threats or get angry, but make it clear that your friendly relationship cannot continue if the situation is not resolved. Let your neighbor know that you will not be upset if the item is lost or damaged, but you do expect that it be replaced or that compensation be provided.

■ Chalk It Up to an Expensive Life Lesson

While you are well within your rights to take legal action to get your stuff back, the expense required in time, money, and energy will almost certainly outweigh the reward of being reunited with your circular saw, garden hose, curling iron, or whatever else you lent your neighbor. At the end of the day, having to buy a replacement is a small price to pay for the knowledge that you live next door to a thief.

My Hard Drive Failed

Likelihood of Happening: Moderate
Ease of Prevention: Low
Is Time a Factor? No

We treat modern computers in a way that's very similar to how most people have always treated their cars. As long as it's working today, we assume it will be working tomorrow. And the day after that. And the day after that. But just like when our car's alternator is on the fritz, most people have absolutely no idea what to do when their laptop's hard drive calls it quits, which can be particularly terrifying in a day and age where entire manuscripts, collections of family photos, and important financial information are just a small mechanical failure away from being lost forever.

■ Rule Out Other Issues

Just because you can't access your files, that doesn't necessarily mean there's a problem with your hard drive. Your internal drive is just one of many components inside your computer that could be causing the problem. In order to determine for sure whether your hard drive has a problem, you'll need a second, fully functioning computer and a universal hard drive adapter.

First, remove the hard drive from the computer that's experiencing problems. The process will be different for each machine, so check your owner's manual or look for video tutorials online. Once the hard drive is free, connect it to the universal hard drive adapter—which you can usually purchase online for around thirty dollars—and plug the adapter into your secondary computer. If you are able to read the drive, then your issue is with your computer and not your hard drive. If that is the case, take this opportunity to transfer all of your files onto the secondary computer. If you still can't access the files on the drive, then you likely have a problem with the hard drive itself.

Hope You Have a Mac

If you suspect your hard drive has failed on a Mac computer, the process for diagnosing the problem does not require you to remove it first. Simply connect your computer to another Mac with a FireWire cable—or using a FireWire adapter if your Mac does not support FireWire—and hold down the T key as you turn on the malfunctioning computer. If the hard drive is functioning, your files should be accessible from the working Mac.

■ Determine How Much the Files Are Worth

At this stage, you have a decision to make. Do you give up and throw the drive in the trash, or do you do everything in your power to resurrect the malfunctioning one? How you answer this question will mostly depend on what's on there.

If the files on your drive consist mostly of old term papers and music you haven't listened to since 2003, then it might not be worth the money or effort to recover them. This is especially true if the files themselves are backed up elsewhere, either on external drives or on cloud storage. If, however, your hard drive holds important information like sensitive work documents or priceless family photos, it might be worth the attempt to get them back.

■ Call in the Pros

While there is software available that can help you retrieve files in the event of a logical failure, your best better is to hire professionals if you are not particularly computer savvy. Unfortunately, data recovery services do not run cheap. Most likely, recovering the information on your drive will set you back a few hundred dollars, and possibly even several thousand. You will also likely need to mail the drive out and wait several days or weeks before you get it back. And once you do have all your precious photos and spreadsheets back in your possession, hopefully this time you'll be so nervous about losing them that you'll back them up in no fewer than ten places.

I Move to a New City and Don't Know Anybody

- **Likelihood of Happening:** Moderate
- **Ease of Prevention:** Low
- **Is Time a Factor?** No

There's a lot to be said for making a fresh start. It's an opportunity to reinvent yourself from the ground up and distance yourself from any unpleasantness from the past. That said, getting settled hundreds or thousands of miles away from home can be difficult if the only person you know in town is the real estate agent who just handed you the keys to your apartment.

■ Get Out and About

When you move to a new city, you suddenly realize just how dependent you are on other people when it comes to finding an excuse to leave the house. After all, it's not often that the average person goes out for dinner, heads to a museum, or simply takes a walk in the park alone. But if you want to meet new people, you'll have to do exactly that.

Take every opportunity to get out in public, and start to think of your home as a place solely for sleeping. Now is not the time to be shy. If you encounter a group of people engaged in an activity you enjoy—like watching a football game at a bar, for example—don't hesitate to politely ask if you can join in. The worst that could happen is they say no.

■ Participate in Organized Activities

Making friends was much easier when you were a kid, and part of that was because you were constantly moving from soccer practice to dance lessons to karate class. You immediately shared common ground with the other kids involved in your activities, and friendships formed organically.

You are all grown up now, but there are still plenty of organized activities geared toward adults. If you are athletically inclined, sign up for a recreational sports league or register for some workout classes. If you prefer sedentary activities, keep an eye out for meet-ups that coincide with your own interests. There's also no reason why you can't try something completely new.

■ Make Friends at Work

Whether you work in a large office or a small one, there are bound to be a few people around with whom you share common interests. Start by inviting a small group of your coworkers out to lunch to get everyone out of the office. While you are out, do your best to shift the conversation away from work and toward your personal interests or other things that might progress your relationship from coworkers to friends. If all goes well, suggest that you go out for drinks after work sometime. As time goes on and you feel more comfortable with everyone, plan a party or suggest other activities outside of work. Before you know it, you will have successfully made the leap from people who share a workspace to longtime friends.

If you don't have a job, or work from home, consider volunteering at a local animal shelter or any charity you would like to support. Many volunteers return regularly, and there's a good chance you'll be able to foster several meaningful friendships.

My Relative Is a Hoarder

— **Likelihood of Happening:** Moderate
— **Ease of Prevention:** Low
— **Is Time a Factor?** No

There's nothing wrong with collecting a few keepsakes here and there—everybody does it. A few boxes of comic books, old birthday cards, or American Girl dolls are nothing to freak out about. But if you are greeted with mountains of old newspapers and piles of sugar packets every time you walk through your relative's door, she might just have a problem.

◾ Be Supportive, not Embarrassed

The compulsion to hoard is a psychological disorder experienced by as many as 5 percent of adults. Keep in mind that your uncle, parents, or grandparents are not purposely trying to upset you with their actions. They may very well be aware of the irrationality of refusing to part with the contents of their home, but are unable to bring themselves to change their behavior.

Before you can help your loved ones, you need to determine if there is actually a problem. If your relative is a compulsive hoarder, you may notice:

- They hold onto things most people would throw away.
- Important areas of the home, like beds, kitchens, and bathrooms, are rendered inaccessible due to excessive clutter.
- Trash and food waste make the home unhygienic.

- The number of pets present in the home exceeds the ability of your loved one to provide them with adequate care.

Your loved ones may go to great lengths to hide the extent of their hoarding from you, so you may need to infringe on their privacy and snoop around in order to verify the severity of the problem.

Get Professional Help

The best way to help your loved ones manage their disorder is to convince them to seek medical treatment. While psychologists are just beginning to understand the nature of the disorder, many have experienced some success with several forms of treatment, including:

- **Drug Therapy:** Several antidepressants have been shown to significantly reduce the symptoms of hoarding disorder in patients.
- **Cognitive-Behavioral Therapy:** A doctor may recommend that your relative see a therapist to help uncover the underlying cause of the hoarding behavior. The therapist may also help your relative identify things that trigger hoarding behavior, and work to manage them.
- **In-Home Therapy:** A therapist and/or a professional organizer may want to come to your relative's home to work on organizing the clutter and prioritizing items to keep and discard. While this may not successfully eliminate the hoarding compulsion, it can help to make the home more livable.

It's important to understand that your loved one may never be completely free of the compulsion to hoard. However, any one or a combination of these therapy methods can significantly increase quality of life.

■ Be Honest

If your family member refuses to seek professional help, it is important to be honest about how the hoarding behavior affects your relationship. The goal is not to upset or shame your relative, but instead to draw attention to the negative aspects of hoarding behavior. She may see it as harmless, and not have considered the health dangers or risk of injury that can occur due to the state of the home.

While you shouldn't go so far as to forcefully declutter your relative's living space, you can offer to help them by reorganizing things. You may find that they are more receptive to the idea of discarding things when they aren't forced to make all of the difficult decisions.

While you won't be able to solve your relative's hoarding problems on your own, you can at least be supportive until she is ready to get the necessary help.

My Cats Don't Get Along

- **Likelihood of Happening:** High
- **Ease of Prevention:** Low
- **Is Time a Factor?** No

Conventional wisdom states that cats are solitary creatures that occasionally mimic affectionate behavior to procure food and shelter from unwitting humans. So perhaps it should come as no surprise that many felines are less than thrilled to share their space with the new companion you've brought home from the shelter. But while they might never be best friends, there are steps you can take to keep things civil.

■ Give Them a Second Chance at a First Impression

If, when the first time your kitties met, you simply unlocked the cat carrier and watched what happened, it's no surprise the result was reminiscent of a gladiator battle. To keep the fur from flying, take a more subtle approach for their reintroduction.

First, divide your house into two distinct territories, so that there is at least one closed door separating the two animals. If this is not possible, then simply isolate one of the cats in a spare bedroom, office, or other room. Each territory will need to contain all of the essentials, such as food, water, toys, and a litter box.

Let the cats roam throughout their respective areas, and be sure to provide them with equal amounts of affection and stimulation. After a few days, swap the territories so each cat has the chance to scent mark the opposite territory. Once they seem comfortable, gradually integrate the two territories by opening all the doors and setting up baby gates. Allow the cats to "share" meals at opposite sides of the gate, and eventually you should be able to remove the boundaries entirely.

■ Break Up the Fight

Once everyone is reacquainted—and hopefully behaving—you'll need to continue some of the practices you established when you had them in separate areas. Providing them with two litter boxes, two food/water bowls, and multiple toys and scratching posts will cut down on territorial disputes.

If fights do arise, you can break them up by keeping a spray bottle full of water on hand and spritzing them to send them scurrying to their separate corners. If you are averse to this method, stomping your feet or clapping your hands may also yield the desired effect.

■ Turn Your Home Into a Cat Paradise

If your cats still aren't getting along, it might have more to do with the layout of your home than their conflicting personalities. Cats feel safest when they have plenty of enclosed hiding places to duck into. These can take the form of cardboard boxes strewn throughout the house or homemade kitty fortresses constructed of blankets hung over chairs. There are also plenty of retail options, like dedicated cat tents that offer more permanent solutions.

Try to think vertically, not just horizontally, when you are pimping out your home. Being up high allows both cats to survey the terrain below, making them feel less anxious about a potential ambush. Consider purchasing a cat tree, or simply make room on bookshelves and on top of dressers. Once both of your cats feel safe and secure at home, they'll slowly start to make friends—or at least have enough room to stay out of each other's way.

I'm Lost in a Foreign Country

Likelihood of Happening: Moderate
Ease of Prevention: High
Is Time a Factor? Yes

Being lost in your home country can be embarrassing, but generally speaking it's not a big deal. You may have to impose on some people more familiar with the area, but you should be on your way after just a few minutes. However, if you find yourself stuck in a remote area of Peru and don't speak a word of Spanish, that's a different story.

■ Head for Tourist Traps

While it's unlikely anyone at the local laundromat is going to speak fluent English—although it's possible—you might have better luck at local restaurants, hotels, or any businesses that commonly cater to tourists. Even if you can't track down anyone with whom you can communicate, you might be able to pick up a map or travel guide in English to help you get your bearings.

Alternatively, you may be able to simply hop into a cab and leave the conversation at nothing more than the destination. Proper names often don't translate well from one language to another, so stating the name of your hotel upon entering the cab might just be enough. Just be sure the vehicle you are getting into is a licensed taxi.

■ Use Expressions and Hand Gestures

Every culture is different, but there are a few human gestures that are pretty common in most spots across the globe. With few exceptions, nodding your head means yes, shaking it means no, and smiling is a sign of friendliness. Pointing one's finger is almost sure to mean "that way."

Nothing Is Universal

Before you jump to the immediate conclusion that a thumbs up indicates you've done something right, take a moment to consider where you are in the world. For example, Bulgarians shake their heads from left to right for yes and nod up for no. In some parts of India, a back and forth head bobble can mean everything from "yes," to "maybe," to "I heard what you said, but don't want to say yes or no."

With that in mind, scrape together what little linguistic ability you have and combine it with rudimentary gestures to convey to a local that you are lost and explain where you need to go. Having a map here can be especially helpful, but you can always ask your new friend to draw you a rudimentary one if there's pen and paper nearby.

■ Let Your Phone Speak for You

You may not have progressed beyond "hello" and "thank you" when it comes to mastering the local dialect, but there are plenty of online services that can make up for that shortcoming. If you have access to the Internet from your phone—be prepared for exorbitant international charges—you can use a translator to look up simple phrases to help you ask for directions.

Depending on how sophisticated your phone is, you may even be able to find an app that will allow you to have a real-time conversation with someone where you ask questions in English and the phone translates them to the native language, and vice versa.

There's a Mouse in My House

— **Likelihood of Happening:** High
— **Ease of Prevention:** Moderate
— **Is Time a Factor?** No

The best time to encounter a mouse is when it's bouncing around inside a glass aquarium at your local pet store. You might even think to yourself, "What a cute little creature." But when it's scurrying across your kitchen floor and nibbling its way through your pantry, "adorable" is the last adjective you'd use to describe the pesky vermin.

■ Find Out Where Your Mouse Lives

You may have seen your unwelcome houseguest scrambling across the living room, but that doesn't mean he settles down each night underneath your coffee table. Mice tend to make their nests in remote, dark areas of homes, so check in closets, behind large appliances, or anywhere that you don't commonly frequent. Keep an eye out for clumps of tattered clothing, paper, or other scraps that the mouse has used to construct a nest. Also pay close attention to any strange smells you may encounter, as nests tend to give off a musty odor. Mouse droppings, which take the form of small black or grey pellets, are another sure indicator that your furry friend's home is nearby.

■ Set a Trap

Selecting a method for dealing with your mouse problem is a moral decision, and one you will need to come to on your own. Each has its own advantages and disadvantages:

- **Live Traps:** There are a number of mousetraps that take the "catch and release" approach to dealing with mice. They can be relatively expensive, but most are reusable. You will have to take the extra step of relocating your mouse to a nearby field, but the reward for your efforts is disposing of a live mouse instead of a dead one. If you are releasing live mice, be sure to do so at least a mile away from your home. Simply dumping them in the backyard is going to send them scurrying right back inside the first chance they get.
- **Deadly Traps:** The iconic snap trap, sticky glue traps, and sophisticated electrocuting traps are all designed to kill mice. Some do so instantly, like the snap trap, while others rely on trapping the mouse

in one place until it starves or you euthanize it yourself. These types of traps can be very inexpensive, but you will inevitably need to dispose of the deceased animal.

- **Poison:** Generally administered in pellet form, poisons work in a number of different ways, but the outcome is always the same: dead mice. While cheap and able to wipe out large infestations relatively quickly, the poisons can be dangerous to household pets if ingested. They can take several days to work, so there's also the nasty business of tracking down the carcasses later.

Depending on your preferred method of extermination—or relocation—you will either take the shotgun approach of placing a large number of traps throughout your home or opt for a more strategic method. In either case, congregate the majority of your traps in places where you've noticed excessive droppings or near the area where you believe the nest(s) to be.

Be sure to check your traps frequently, as a mouse carcass can attract flies and start to smell over time. This also applies to humane traps, which can devolve into torture chambers if the mouse has to go too long without food.

■ Keep Your Home Mouse-Free

Now that you've eliminated your furry friend(s), take a few precautionary measures to prevent future infestations. Seal up any holes or cracks near your doors, walls, and windows that lead outside. If the weather is warm, pay special attention to door and window screens that may have holes large enough for mice to squeeze through. You can also purchase various natural and chemical repellants to place around areas you feel mice might be using to gain access to your home.

My Houseguest Just Won't Leave

- **Likelihood of Happening:** High
- **Ease of Prevention:** High
- **Is Time a Factor?** Yes

When your old college roommate asked to crash on your couch for a few days, you thought it would be fun. You'd stay up late playing video games, reminisce about the good old days, and catch up on how much your lives have changed over the years. But as days turn to weeks—or even months—you find yourself more concerned with when your living room will convert back to a sitting area instead of a motel.

■ Set a Firm Deadline

While you may feel a reasonable timeframe for departure has already come and gone, it's quite possible you weren't clear at the outset how long you were willing to let your friend stay. Certainly you would never presume to overstay your welcome if the situation was reversed, but there are some people who will take the phrase "stay as long as you'd like" quite literally.

The next time you are alone with your friend, make it very clear that you've enjoyed all the time you've spent together lately, but you will need the place to yourself again soon. Give a firm date, be it a few days or a few weeks in the future, whatever you are comfortable with. Allow your friend the opportunity to explain his side of the story, too. It's quite possible he simply doesn't have any other options.

■ Help Out with the Next Steps

You aren't a landlord, but you aren't a monster, either. The last thing you want is to kick your friend to the curb with nowhere else to go. As your agreed-upon deadline approaches, do your best to help your friend secure a new place to stay. If money is an issue, you will have to decide for yourself whether you feel comfortable offering a loan. Keep in mind that you are merely offering your assistance. Whether it's finding a new job or tracking down an affordable one-bedroom, your friend needs to be the driving force here.

Beware Squatters' Rights

Depending on what state your guest is in—physically, not philosophically—he may be considered a legitimate tenant after a certain period of time. As such, you might have to begin a formal eviction process in order to get him to leave.

■ Don't Be an Enabler

If your houseguest continues to take advantage of your hospitality, perhaps you should stop being so hospitable. If you continue to provide meals, laundry, Internet, and cleaning services for your friend at a cost of zero dollars a night, no alternative will ever be even remotely enticing.

At mealtimes, make it clear that you have only prepared food for yourself and you expect your friend to see to his own needs. Start keeping the detergent and any other items you don't want your guest using locked away during the day. Unplug your modem and bring it with you when you go to work. Anything to make your home seem less appealing.

Hopefully your unwelcome guest will get the hint and mosey on over to the local Best Western soon. But if all else fails, you can always have the police escort your now former buddy off the premises.

I'm about to Miss a Flight

- **Likelihood of Happening:** Moderate
- **Ease of Prevention:** High
- **Is Time a Factor?** Yes

Conventional wisdom states that you should arrive at the airport at least two hours before your flight. Almost everybody aims to do exactly that. But by the time you've packed your bags, stopped for lunch, taken the dog to the kennel, messed around on your phone for a bit, and stood for an eternity trying to hail a cab, that two-hour cushion begins to dwindle rapidly.

■ Get the Details En Route

As you rush to the airport and try to head your plane off at the pass, you could use the time to anxiously bite your nails and curse yourself for being late, or you could do something useful with the time you have. There are a number of crucial pieces of information you will need about your flight once you get to the terminal, but there's no reason to wait that long to gather it all in one place.

Before you even set foot in the airport, use your phone to look up the terminal, flight status (hopefully it's delayed), and often the gate number for your flight. Some airlines will even let you check in from your phone, which could save you valuable minutes of waiting in line.

■ Speed Through Security

See that massive line forming at the entrance to the terminal? That's the TSA security checkpoint, and it's your biggest hurdle for making it to your destination. While you can't skip it entirely, you can take a few measures to get through the process more quickly.

First and foremost, take a moment to explain your situation to a TSA agent and see if she can move you to the front of the line or send you through the speedier Precheck lane. Who knows, you might catch her on a good day.

If that fails, then you can save yourself a lot of time by disposing of any prohibited items from your carry-on prior to entering the line. The list of no-nos includes sharp objects, flammable materials, most weapons, and liquids greater than 3.4 ounces. When you're running late, the last thing you need is to get a private patdown over a bottle of water. Also, be sure to have your ID and boarding pass ready and remove your shoes, belt, coat, and any metal objects before you get to the front of the line.

■ Invoke the Flat-Tire Rule

Despite all the frenzied disrobing and frantic running, you still might not make it to the gate in time. So you are either going to have to skip out on that trip to Tahiti, or pay through the nose to rebook the flight last minute. Or will you?

Many airlines have either official or unofficial policies in place to waive the rebooking fees as well as any fare differential for the next available flight if a customer missed the original flight by less than two hours due to reasons beyond his control. When it comes time to plead your case, just make sure to come up with something better than "My niece posted the cutest cat video ever to Facebook and I lost track of time."

My Tattoo Artist Screwed Up

- **Likelihood of Happening:** Low
- **Ease of Prevention:** High
- **Is Time a Factor?** No

With at least 23 percent of Americans sporting some form of ink, and cultures around the world incorporating the practice into their traditional standards of beauty, tattoos clearly aren't just for sailors anymore. With a couple of bucks and a few hours of pain, anyone can have a beautiful work of art permanently etched on any portion of their body. Unfortunately, you can also have a complete disaster permanently etched on any portion of your body if your artist's work is less than stellar.

■ Don't Get Mad—Yet

There are a number of reasons why your finished tattoo might not meet your expectations. If something is misspelled, perhaps neither you nor the artist took the time to read through the text carefully. If the colors are off, you might just need to wait a while for the skin to heal before everything looks the way it should. You may have moved at an inopportune moment, causing the artist to slip. But beyond making sure it doesn't happen again, the cause of the screwup doesn't matter. What matters is getting it fixed.

Tattoo artists rely very heavily on word of mouth for marketing, so it is in your artist's best interest to ensure you are satisfied with your experience. If you explain what about the tattoo you are uncomfortable with, your artist should be able to walk you through various options for rectifying the issue.

■ Turn Lemons Into Lemonade

Sure, your arm might say "Wow" instead of "Mom" right now, but it doesn't have to stay that way forever. Depending on the location, size, and color of the tattoo, your artist might be able to hide the mistake with clever shading or by reworking the entire piece from the ground up. Regardless of what solution you choose, however, be absolutely certain you and the artist are on the same page before you move forward.

If you aren't comfortable allowing the original artist to perform the touchups, you can shop around and find other artists in the area who might be better suited to the task. You might even discover that the artist who first worked on your piece is notorious for screwups, and you are not the first person to go shopping around for a fix.

■ Start over from Scratch

Tattoos have never been truly permanent, but the options for removing them have traditionally been rather unappealing. Small tattoos could be removed surgically, but scarring was more or less unavoidable. For larger tattoos, gradually scraping away the layers of dyed skin in a process known as dermabrasion could do the trick, but this could also lead to widespread scarring.

Today, the preferred method is laser removal, where a specialist uses lasers calibrated to isolate pigments and break down the ink so that the body can absorb it. The procedure is costly, however, and may require multiple sessions spread out over several months to fully eliminate the tattoo—if it's even possible to do so. Depending on the color of your skin as well as that of the tattoo, complete laser removal might not be possible. But, if all else fails, you can always embrace your little blunder and insist that you always intended for it to look that way.

My Dog Ate Chocolate

- **Likelihood of Happening:** Moderate
- **Ease of Prevention:** High
- **Is Time a Factor?** Yes

Dogs may be relatively intelligent when compared to other members of the animal kingdom, but when it comes to food, they simply don't have the good sense to steer clear of things that could cause them harm. And when it comes to dangerous foods, chocolate is near the top of the list.

■ Take Immediate Action

Depending on the size of your dog and the type of chocolate it consumed, even as little as an ounce can prove fatal if left untreated. In general, the situation becomes more severe the smaller the dog and the darker the chocolate. Dogs have trouble metabolizing a chemical called theobromine, which is present in relatively large quantities in dark chocolate and relatively low quantities in white chocolate. Symptoms of theobromine poisoning in dogs include hyperactivity, dehydration, agitation, vomiting, diarrhea, tachycardia, seizures, and sometimes death. To give your pooch the best chance for survival, most vets recommend you take immediate action if you have any reason to suspect your animal may have ingested chocolate.

■ Induce Vomiting

If you are relatively certain your dog has only just recently consumed chocolate (within the past two hours), then your best option is to induce vomiting. One surefire method is to feed your dog a small amount of hydrogen peroxide, approximately one teaspoon for every 10 pounds he weighs. If your dog refuses to ingest it, you can mix it with water or honey to make it more appetizing.

Once you've gotten the hydrogen peroxide into your dog's system, take him for a fifteen-minute walk to allow time for it to irritate his gastrointestinal tract and induce vomiting. This also ensures that the resulting mess occurs outside rather than on your floor. If your dog doesn't vomit, you can administer a second and final dose. If your dog still won't vomit, you will need to call a vet.

■ Visit the Doggie ER

If your dog won't expel the chocolate on his own, or if it's been longer than two hours since he ingested it, then you will need to take your pet immediately to the vet. If your usual vet is not open, don't wait to make an appointment until the following day. Instead, rush your animal immediately to the closest open clinic. Once there, the vet will evaluate your dog and take one of several measures which may include:

- Administering activated charcoal
- Prescribing anti-vomiting medication
- Providing fluids via an IV
- Prescribing heart medication to counter the damage done by the chocolate

As long as you've gotten your pooch to the vet within a reasonable timeframe, the prognosis is good for a speedy recovery.

My Significant Other's Parents Hate Me

- **Likelihood of Happening:** Moderate
- **Ease of Prevention:** Moderate
- **Is Time a Factor?** No

The first time you met your boyfriend or girlfriend's parents as a teenager, you almost expected that they weren't going to be particularly fond of you. Fortunately, after you endured a tour of his or her dad's gun collection, you were probably able to avoid the parents for the duration of the relationship. But as you get older, it becomes increasingly essential to have the approval of your future—or present—in-laws, and increasingly frustrating if you can't gain their respect.

■ Look Inward, not Outward

When we can't seem to get along with someone, our natural tendency is to focus on what's wrong with him or her. After all, you think you are a good person, so if someone else doesn't agree then they must be the one with the problem.

While it may be a difficult exercise, take a moment to reflect on anything about your personality or behavior that might be clashing with their values. If you always order a glass of wine with dinner and they stick with water, perhaps they have negative views on alcohol. If you have conflicting political views, maybe they don't appreciate the frequency with which you bring up sensitive subjects. Even if the potential issues you discover can't be easily changed—or you don't want to change them—you can still make it a point to tone them down when you are around your significant other's family.

■ Find Common Ground

Even if your significant other comes from a conservative Christian family who love Sunday afternoon football and you're a staunch atheist who has never so much as played a game of catch, there's bound to be something you have in common. Use your significant other as your greatest ally and pick his or her brain for activities you can organize that everyone will appreciate.

Stick to things you feel comfortable doing, and don't overextend yourself. If you pretend to be an avid golfer but can't even hit the ball off the tee, you are only going to solidify their distaste for you.

■ Have a Heart-to-Heart

A large part of why you can't seem to get along with your significant other's parents could be that they just don't know enough about you. This can be especially true if your better half has a habit of complaining to them about your faults without highlighting the things he or she loves about you.

Pick a time when your significant other is out of town or busy with friends and invite the parents out for lunch or a drink so they can get to know you better. If things are going well, you might even want to broach the fact that they have taken a while to warm up to you. Assure them that you have nothing but the best intentions for their son or daughter and that you hope you can earn their trust in time. If they still aren't convinced, don't get discouraged and give up. Keep at it, and sooner or later their walls will break down and they will learn to like you—or at the very least accept you.

I'm Trapped in an Elevator

- **Likelihood of Happening:** Low
- **Ease of Prevention:** Moderate
- **Is Time a Factor?** Yes

How many times have you walked by an elevator and noticed a sign indicating that it's temporarily out of order? When you are forced to take the stairs, the lack of automated transportation is little more than a minor nuisance. If, however, the elevator decides to wait until you are in the middle of using it to malfunction, the situation becomes a little more severe.

■ Leave No Button Unpressed

You are currently stuck, and no amount of button mashing is going to make that worse. You might, however, find that the doors are merely jammed shut and that pressing either the "door open" or "door close" buttons will fix the problem. Similarly, the button for the floor you selected might be on the fritz, and selecting another floor could get the elevator moving again.

Placebo Buttons

Ever impatiently press the close-door button on an elevator and wonder why it's so slow to respond? That could be because it doesn't even work. Similar to the little buttons found at crosswalks, the close-door button in many elevators is in place simply to act as a placebo and make the user believe her actions are changing the outcome.

▦ Be Patient

If you can't get the doors open on your own and you are able to call for help on a cell phone or by using the emergency communication system inside the elevator, then your best bet is to take a few deep breaths, sit down on the floor, and wait for the cavalry to arrive. Even if you can't get through to anyone on the outside right away, someone else in need of the elevator might discover it is out of order shortly. You may also be able to get someone's attention by banging on the walls of the elevator.

If none of the buttons work, you can't contact anyone outside, and you are absolutely certain that nobody is coming to help you, then you may need to escape on your own.

▦ Try to Escape on Your Own

Keep in mind that attempting to escape from a disabled elevator is a very risky proposition—so safety first. Before you do anything, make sure the emergency stop switch is engaged in case the elevator springs back to life while you are fumbling around in the shaft.

Next, attempt to pry open the doors with your hands or any objects you have with you in the elevator. If you succeed and the elevator isn't stuck between floors, then you are all set to go. If you find yourself between floors and the distance is too great to safely reach, then you'll need to locate the service hatch on the ceiling and make your way onto the top of the elevator. Be careful of any exposed wiring, and limit the time that you spend up there. Once you are on top of the elevator, you should be able to reach the open doorway leading to the floor above you.

Once out, you should immediately alert someone in the building of the issue so that the elevator can be serviced, and nobody else finds themself in the same unfortunate situation from which you just escaped.

My Air Conditioner Fails in the Middle of Summer

Likelihood of Happening: Moderate
Ease of Prevention: Low
Is Time a Factor? No

There are few things more amazing than feeling your house transition from a sweltering, 100°F sweatbox to a luxurious, 70°F heaven on earth. And there are few things worse than hearing the air conditioner conk out and feeling the temperature slowly tick back up.

■ Keep the Cool Air In and the Hot Air Out

If you are in the middle of a heat wave, chances are slim that you'll be able to track down an AC unit at the store or find someone to come repair the busted one right away. So until it's fixed or replaced, you are on your own.

In the short term, close all the curtains to keep out the sunlight and prevent the warm air outside from entering through cracks. If you don't have curtains, tinfoil taped to the windows can also be very effective.

■ Don't Create More Heat

Your stove and oven are two obvious generators of heat, so avoid cooking anything if at all possible. If you must warm something up, your microwave will give off far less heat than your other options. You can also take this as an opportunity to fire up the grill, if you are willing to brave the outdoors and sacrifice your own comfort for the sake of your family's. You should also avoid using other heat-generating devices in your home like big-screen televisions, desktop computers, and high-wattage lights.

■ Bring Out All the Fans

If you have desktop fans and window fans, now's the time to get them out of the closet and set them up. If you have a freezer full of ice, place shallow bowls of ice water in front of the fans to create cool air that is then blown around the room. This can be surprisingly effective if you have enough ice to keep the water cold.

As for ceiling fans, make sure they are set to run counter-clockwise. If they spin clockwise, they will push warm air down—which is the last thing you want.

■ Make It Through the Night

When the sun goes down and the temperature drops, it's safe to crack open the windows and get some cooler outside air flowing throughout the house. You can also reposition your fans so they rest in the window frame to maximize the amount of cool air circulating from outside.

If you are having trouble sleeping, you can soak a thin T-shirt with water and wear it in bed. The evaporation should keep you cool for a few hours. You can get the same effect by wetting a thin sheet and draping it over yourself.

If the heat is completely unbearable, you could also move down to sleep on the first floor or even in the basement, and cross your fingers that the repairman will be able to make it in the morning.

I Locked My Keys in My Car

— **Likelihood of Happening:** Moderate
— **Ease of Prevention:** High
— **Is Time a Factor?** No

On the list of "things that make you feel like an idiot," getting locked out of your own car sits near the top. It's even worse if you managed to lock your cell phone inside as well. While this is rarely a life-threatening situation, if you find yourself stranded in a bad neighborhood or the weather takes a turn for the worse, you will want to rectify your blunder quickly.

■ Keep Calm and Double Check

Take the number of doors in your car and subtract it from the number of doors you've tried to open. If that number doesn't equal zero, then there's still a chance you aren't quite as locked out as you think you are. Also be sure to check the trunk, as it might be possible to push the seats down and reach your keys or unlock the doors that way.

■ Head to the Nearest Drugstore

If you are within walking distance of a pharmacy or you can catch a cab, there are a few items you need to pick up:

- Metal coat hanger
- Blood pressure cuff

Once you are back at your car, untwist the top of the hanger and bend it until you have a long poking tool.

Next, firmly grasp the driver-side door handle and pull the door out until a ¼-inch gap forms. With your other hand, slip the cuff into the gap. Once it is lodged in place, squeeze the bulb to pump the cuff with air until you are able to widen the gap to at least ½ inch, preferably 1 inch. Just be careful not to stress the door too much, as this might cause the window to crack. Once the gap is large enough, snake the wire hanger down the side into the car and depress the unlock button or hook the lock knob or pin and pull it up. If you weren't able to track down a hanger, a thin stick may also work.

Peel back the weather stripping at the base of the window and insert your poking tool of choice between the window and the stripping. Once you've lowered a few inches, you can start moving it around to feel for the locking pin, which should be located close to the inside door handle. Once you've located it, gently pull it toward the trunk of the car to unlock the car.

If you can't break in via the driver's side door, you might have better luck on the passenger's side. Oftentimes the locking mechanism of the passenger door is less complicated than the one on the driver's side door, and you can use this to your advantage.

I Lost My Passport in a Foreign Country

- **Likelihood of Happening:** Moderate
- **Ease of Prevention:** High
- **Is Time a Factor?** Yes

If you lose your camera, traveler's checks, or phone while traveling abroad, you might come home with a harrowing story of roadside robbery, but at least you'll come home. Lose your passport however, and you are absolutely 100 percent stuck.

But thankfully, not forever.

■ Go Straight to the Embassy

The U.S. government operates some 253 embassies and consulates spread across every country with which the United States maintains diplomatic relations. Once you are certain your passport is missing, your first step to getting back home is to find the nearest embassy and make a beeline for it.

Once at the embassy, they will be able to help you file a police report if the passport was stolen. If the passport was simply lost or damaged and there was no criminal activity, the embassy can get you started on the process of issuing your replacement passport.

■ Call for Reinforcements

In order to secure a replacement passport, you will need to prove you are who you say you are. If you were prepared, you photocopied your passport and driver's license before you left and already have them with you. If not, you are going to have to phone a friend in the United States to track down the following:

- Identification (driver's license or expired passport)
- Proof of citizenship (birth certificate, naturalization certificate, certificate of citizenship)

Usually faxed copies of these documents are sufficient, and it is not necessary to mail them overseas.

While your U.S. contact is frantically searching for your documents, you want to find a place to take your new passport photos. There is very specific criterion for passport photos, and it's likely the embassy will not have the necessary equipment to produce them. Your passport needs to be:

- 2×2 inches
- Taken within the last six months
- Printed on photo paper
- Full face, front view on white or off-white background
- Between 1 inch and 1⅜ inches from the bottom of the chin to the top of the head
- Neutral facial expression with both eyes open

If all goes according to plan, you should have your replacement passport in your hands within a matter of hours after visiting the embassy. And when you leave, make sure it stays there . . .

■ Take Better Care of Your New Passport

Citizens who "lose" multiple passports in a short period of time raise suspicion with the Department of Homeland Security, so you want to keep your new passport close at hand. If you apply for two replacement passports in a single trip, you may be suspected of providing terrorist organizations with your documentation to help them sneak into the United States. While you will still be allowed to apply for another replacement passport, the process will not be as quick and your application will be scrutinized more heavily.

My Pet Goes Missing

- **Likelihood of Happening:** Moderate
- **Ease of Prevention:** Moderate
- **Is Time a Factor?** Yes

Losing a pet can be a terrifying experience for the owner, and even more so for the animal. But the good news is that the majority of pet owners are eventually reunited with their companions—93 percent for dogs and 75 percent for cats. Here's how to ensure you don't fall into the small group of owners who aren't so lucky.

■ Form a Search Party

If your pet has only been missing for a short time, it's quite likely he is still close to home. Gather up as many friends, neighbors, and family members as you can muster and scour the neighborhood. Split up to cover more ground, and make sure every group has a familiar toy or other item that produces a welcoming sound (like a bag of treats that you can shake). This is likely to be more effective than simply calling the animal's name—especially in the case of cats, which rarely come when called.

For dogs, the issue at hand is how far could he have gone. Depending on how long your pup has been missing, you will need to search a radius of at least two miles—which is a lot of ground to cover. For cats, especially those of the indoor persuasion, the question is more likely where he is hiding? A scared cat isn't likely to bolt out into the open, preferring instead to remain under cover.

Leave Your Scent

Dogs have an incredible sense of smell, and you can use this to help coax your lost pet back home. Find a recently worn article of clothing and lay it on the ground next to where your dog was last seen, alongside a water dish. Your dog will be drawn to the comforting scent and will hopefully curl up to wait for you, so check back frequently.

◼ Visit Local Shelters and Vets

Even if your pet has tags with your address and phone number, there's no guarantee that they won't be lost or damaged after he goes missing. If a Good Samaritan, police officer, or animal control officer picks him up, there's a chance he will end up in a shelter or at a vet. And that's a very good thing.

When you make the rounds of local shelters and vet offices, be sure to bring a photo of your pet to leave with the staff so they can keep an eye out for him. It may be several days before whoever finds him will bring him to the shelter, and a picture is far better than a description when it comes to identifying new arrivals.

If your animal has a microchip embedded beneath its skin—a common practice among modern pet owners—both shelters and vet offices will be equipped to read the information contained on the chip and ensure your animal is returned to you.

◼ Canvass the Neighborhood

If your pet has been missing for a few days, don't give up hope. If you're missing a cat, it's quite possible that someone thinks they have "rescued" a stray rather than found a missing pet. The same could also be true of dogs. To alert everyone in your neighborhood, print out flyers with a clear picture of your pet along with any identifying marks or scars. If you are willing to offer a reward, advertise that in big, bold letters at the top of your flyer. But do not specify the dollar amount of the reward. Too high a number could cause unscrupulous individuals to wonder why your pet is so valuable and may cause them to sell him or keep him for themselves.

You can also post an ad to websites like Craigslist or other local forums, which often have special areas where pet owners can post missing animals. It's also possible that whoever found your animal has made a posting online, so be sure to check out the section for found pets.

I Need to Break Into My House

- **Likelihood of Happening:** Moderate
- **Ease of Prevention:** High
- **Is Time a Factor?** No

Going out to check the mail while your toddler napped may have seemed like a good idea at the time, but now you're trapped outside and there's no telling what kind of trouble he'll get into when he wakes up. Or perhaps you left the oven on, stepped out for a minute, and need to step back in before your pot roast catches fire. There are a dozen reasons why you might need to break into your own home, and not all of them allow for the time it takes to wait for a locksmith.

■ Take a Moment to Think

Before you start smashing windows and breaking down doors, stop and take a look around. Perhaps there's a window you left open somewhere on the first floor, or a ladder in the toolshed you can use to get to the second. How long do you have before the situation inside becomes dire? If there's a risk of fire or personal injury, you may need to call for emergency assistance. If you have time on your side, use it to focus on how to get inside without doing any permanent damage.

■ Bust a Chain Lock

If any of the entrances to your house are latched with nothing more than a chain lock, your indifference to proper home security may help you here. A rubber band and approximately thirty seconds of effort can get you back inside.

Crack the door open slightly and tie the rubber band to the chain closest to the latch to create a loop. Next, secure the loop on the inside door handle—this may require some hand gymnastics—and shut the door. The rubber band should pull the latch and allow you to waltz right in.

■ Use Your Credit Card

Actors in action films have an uncanny ability to bypass any number of security measures with everyday objects, and there's some truth to this trope. Provided your deadbolt isn't engaged, you can open your locked door with a humble credit card. Simply insert the card between the door and the frame just above the latch, and bend it slightly away from the knob as you slide it downward. When you feel the lock give way, turn the knob and pull the door open.

■ Use a Door Window

Just because your door is locked doesn't meant it's impregnable. If your door has windows you should be able to use a flathead screwdriver to remove one fairly easily. Simply insert the screwdriver at the base of one of the panes and wiggle it around while gently pushing down on the handle to exert upward force. The window should come out and allow you to reach down to unlock the door. Just be sure to replace the pane before you leave your house again. You might also want to consider leaving a key with a neighbor for the next time you lock yourself out.

My Home Is Infested with Bed Bugs

- **Likelihood of Happening:** Moderate
- **Ease of Prevention:** Moderate
- **Is Time a Factor?** No

They may be only four millimeters long, but few other insects strike the same level of fear and anxiety in the hearts of tenants and homeowners as the infamous bed bug. And with good reason. They are notoriously difficult to eradicate, with many renters choosing to move rather than face more failed attempts to evict the vampiric pests. Homeowners who don't have that option curse their luck and don't tell their friends about their unwelcome overnight guests. But while you can't deny that a bed bug infestation is a major inconvenience, it doesn't have to end badly if you know what to do.

■ Confirm the Infestation

Bed bugs are small and mostly nocturnal, so the chances are slim that your first indication of a bed bug infestation will be spotting a live critter. Instead, you are far more likely to notice small specks of fecal matter, molted exoskeletons, and of course the telltale red bumps on your skin caused by the bed bugs' bites. The bugs also give off a distinct odor that can allegedly be detected by trained dogs, but the reported success rates for this method are questionable.

■ Deal with Your Bed

Once you've determined you are truly faced with a full-blown bed bug infestation, the first question you'll need to answer is, "How much do I like my bed frame and mattress?" Your whole bed—from the box spring to the bed sheets—is the most likely hangout for the majority of your unwelcome guests, and it is also extremely difficult to treat. If you can easily part with it, your best bet is to throw everything away.

If you are determined to keep it, a bug-proof mattress cover will slowly starve the bed bugs to death, while spot treatment of the frame may be enough to eradicate them there. But even if you treat your bed, you're not done yet . . .

■ Sanitize Everything You Own

This next step may sound like overkill, but it's essential if you want to be certain you have completely eradicated your bed bug infestation. You need to sanitize everything you own. Yes, everything.

Bed bugs like to stay close to their host—meaning you—but by no means are they limited to the bed. You'll need to vacuum your carpets, wipe down every inch of furniture, and even check the cracks in your wood floors for signs of bed bugs and their eggs. Bed bugs can't survive temperatures above 113°F, so clothes and bed linens can usually be treated by washing them in hot water and placing them in the dryer on high heat. Cold temperatures below freezing will also kill the bugs and their eggs, but can take upwards of two weeks to work.

If you can't heat it, freeze it, or clean it, your only other option is to place the item in a sealed plastic bag for six months to starve any live bugs.

■ Call a Professional

A bed bug infestation is not the time for a DIY project. Your home is full of cracks and crevices where bed bugs can hide, and all of your hard work will be for naught if you don't completely eliminate every single trace of them. Professional exterminators are trained to locate bed bug nests and have years of experience removing them from residences, so give them a call. You'll be glad you did.

CHAPTER 5

Embarrassing Events That Make You Want to Crawl Under a Rock

Some people were born without a sense of shame and never bothered to acquire one over time. For the rest of the population, there are hundreds or even thousands of minor things that could make people uncomfortable enough to fake a sudden illness or a death in the family in order to avoid them. If you are in the latter category, it might be wise to try an approach that doesn't involve getting on the next plane to the opposite side of the planet. So read on to find out how to handle many of life's most embarrassing events.

I Have Adult Acne

- **Likelihood of Happening:** Moderate
- **Ease of Prevention:** Low
- **Is Time a Factor?** No

Waking up to a faceful of pimples is an unavoidable reality for many teenagers. While adolescent acne may cause years of embarrassment and leave permanent scars, it generally subsides during the passage into adulthood. For some, however, the constant scrubbing, concealing, and fretting associated with acne extends well into their later years.

■ Get to the Root of the Problem

Pimples don't just erupt on your face at random. Although it may seem like it, they don't pay attention to your calendar and wait for an important interview or a first date to rear their ugly heads. Instead, they are merely a symptom of clogged pores that are filled with built-up bacteria. What causes the pores to become clogged is likely one of the following:

- Overuse of cosmetic products
- Hormonal changes
- Diet
- Stress

In order to stop the onslaught of unsightly red blemishes, you will need to stop treating the pimples themselves and go after the underlying cause.

■ Make Changes to Your Skincare Routine

Adhering to good hygiene practices like routinely washing your face with a mild cleanser is a good start to ridding yourself of adult acne, but the other steps you need to take depend on the other factors causing your breakouts.

- **Overuse of Cosmetic Products:** The oil found in many anti-aging creams and other facial moisturizers can clog pores and lead to breakouts. If you have sensitive skin, look for oil-free products. Failing to completely remove makeup at the end of the day can also contribute to the problem.
- **Hormonal Changes:** Adult acne primarily affects women, and this disparity is mostly due to hormonal changes. To combat the problem, your doctor may be able to prescribe medication to adjust the hormone levels in your body.
- **Diet:** While chocolate and fatty foods have been erroneously linked to acne in the past, new research suggests that high glycemic foods like white bread, pasta, and sugary soft drinks can contribute to flareups. Adjusting your diet may significantly improve your complexion.
- **Stress:** Prolonged stress can cause your body to produce high levels of cortisol, which can throw your other hormones out of whack and lead to breakouts. Make a conscious effort to eliminate the things in your life that cause you stress, or consider yoga or meditation to calm your state of mind.

Everyone's body is different, and any one or a combination of these factors could cause your acne.

◼ See a Dermatologist

Don't presume that every red blemish on your skin is acne. There are several conditions including rosacea, miliaria rubra (a.k.a. prickly heat), folliculitis, and perioral dermatitis that mimic the symptoms of adult acne. If nothing you try seems to make any difference, visit a dermatologist to have your condition evaluated. He should be able to prescribe topical treatments or oral medication to treat the problem.

My Period Strikes Suddenly

Likelihood of Happening: Moderate
Ease of Prevention: Low
Is Time a Factor? Yes

By the time middle school rolls around, most young girls have already been presented with more than they'd like to know about their bodies and how to handle the monthly ritual known as the period. But where in the piles of pamphlets and diagrams is the section on what to do if Aunt Flow pays you a visit at a time when you aren't at all prepared?

◼ Ask for Help

There are very few things that all women can agree on, but one universal truth is that you must provide sanitary products to any woman who requests them—even your worst enemy. No exceptions, no questions asked. It is known. With that in mind, make a beeline for the ladies' room and enlist the aid of the first woman you encounter. If you are at a restaurant with a private bathroom, you may be able to grab someone walking back to her seat or flag down a passing waitress.

■ Construct a DIY Pad

If there's a dearth of women in the restaurant, or you're on a hike instead of at dinner, you are going to need to take care of this on your own. In the event that you are experiencing a light flow or merely spotting, you should be able to get by with a few tissues or some balled-up toilet paper strategically placed in your underwear. If the situation is severe, you can construct a more permanent solution with items you likely have on hand.

First, track down something absorbent you can use to form the base of your makeshift pad. A handful of cotton balls, some gauze from a first-aid kit, thick paper towels, or even a sock will all work in a pinch. Next, generously wrap the absorbent core in toilet paper or tissues and place the pad in your underwear. Finally, wrap several layers of toilet paper or tissues around both underwear and pad. This final step is key, as it prevents the pad from slipping.

■ Hide the Stain, or Own It

Assuming there's no help in sight and there's nothing absorbent within a five-mile radius, then your only option is to discreetly cover up the stain until you return to civilization. If you are wearing dark pants, then you may need do nothing more than avoid sitting on pale-colored fabrics. If you are sporting lighter attire, then you may need to bring back the '90s trend of tying a sweater or jacket around your waist.

If all else fails, you can also spit in the face of societal norms and be open about the situation. At the end of the day, menstruation really isn't something you should feel ashamed of.

My Sex Life Is Dead in the Water

- **Likelihood of Happening:** Moderate
- **Ease of Prevention:** Moderate
- **Is Time a Factor?** No

There's an old saying about marriages that if you were to put a marble in a jar every time you had sex for the first five years and take a marble out every time after, you'd never empty the jar. While this isn't true for everyone, it's an upsetting reality for many couples as the honeymoon phase gives way to a routine that leaves little—if any—time for intimacy. And this can happen whether you've been married for twenty-five years, or you've only been dating six months—and a dip in the frequency of sex can cause a lot of anxiety for both parties.

■ Figure Out If You Really Have a Problem

An important thing to remember about relationships is that no two are the same. For some couples, having sex less than three times a week might be cause for concern. For others, just once a month—or even less—may be more than enough to leave both you and your partner happy. It's up to you to decide how frequent is frequent enough.

That said, when you evaluate the state of your sexual relationship it's important to eliminate any external factors and focus on whether or not you are satisfied. While it's true that life events like having children or getting a promotion at work can take time away from the bedroom, they are no excuse for a sexless marriage.

■ Communicate

Almost any problem in a relationship can be boiled down to a failure to communicate, and trouble in the bedroom is no exception. If you are unhappy with the frequency with which you are intimate—or you think your partner might be—it's healthy to sit down and talk about it. This isn't the time to start an argument or to make accusations; instead, it's an opportunity to have an open and honest discussion.

Keep the conversation light and leave the charts, spreadsheets, and statistics for when it's time to refinance your mortgage. Use the discussion itself as a bridge to rekindle your passion, by taking turns sharing some of the things you would like to change in explicit detail.

■ Make Sex a Priority

As we get older, the day seems to get shorter. Dinner needs to get made, chores need to be done, and kids need to be driven to soccer practice. As a result, sex is often put on the backburner and relegated to an activity that you only share if there's time. In order to maintain a healthy sexual relationship, you may need to schedule romantic evenings the same way you would schedule anything else in your life. It may seem like you are eliminating spontaneity from your relationship, but there's no reason you can't have sex outside of your scheduled time. Setting a dedicated date night merely ensures you won't let your love life take a backseat to everything else you both have on your plates.

■ Address Any Underlying Issues

Sometimes a dead bedroom is more than just an issue with time management, it's a symptom of a larger problem. It could be that one of you has unresolved anger toward the other that needs to be addressed.

Maybe one party has been turned down for sex so often that she feels uncomfortable initiating. There might even be an issue where the sex you do have simply isn't exciting enough. Depending on the issue, you will need to do your best to resolve it on your own, or consider seeking couples counseling or another form of professional help. It's quite possible that there's a medical issue preventing intimacy, in which case there may be medication or other treatment available to alleviate the problem.

I Sexted the Wrong Person

Likelihood of Happening: Moderate
Ease of Prevention: High
Is Time a Factor? No

Modern smartphones may not have invented dirty talk or the nude self-portrait, but they certainly revolutionized the way they're shared. What once required an in-person exchange or a Polaroid camera can now be sent to your long-distance lover in a matter of seconds. Unfortunately, with a slip of the finger, the racy message intended for your significant other can just as easily find its way to your boss.

■ When in Doubt, Blame Your Phone

You can't go so far as to claim your phone became self-aware and started sending provocative text messages on its own, but you can place some of the blame on autocorrect. Phones make strange autocorrections all the time—nobody has ever meant to say they "ducking hate sitting in traffic"—so it's certainly within the realm of possibility. Just be sure to come up with a plausible explanation for what you "meant" to send. There's no phone on earth that is going to change "I'll have those reports to you by Friday" to "I want to be on you."

■ Claim You Were Hacked

Another option is to insist your phone was hacked. Since the majority of people have no real idea what that actually means, you might meet with sympathy rather than disgust.

Go ahead and send a few additional texts or post some strange things to social media to add some believability to your claim. Be careful not to follow up directly from your phone though—since it's "hacked" and all. Also, while this might be enough to persuade grandma, more tech-savvy individuals will likely see through the ruse.

You could also try the slightly more believable story that your phone was outright stolen, but if you go this route you are going to need to replace your case, or possibly even your entire phone, before you see the person again.

■ Own It

If the unintended recipient was a close friend, you might just want to come clean about the situation.

"Yes, I sent you a picture of my butt that was intended for my partner. I apologize if that upset or offended you. On the plus side, at least I wasn't sending you pictures of my butt on purpose."

The truth of the matter is that sexting is something nearly 50 percent of people in relationships indulge in at some point in time. So there's little reason for anyone to be shocked or appalled by it. Now, if your friend sends you a racy response before you have time to explain yourself, then you might have something to worry about.

I Made a Drunken Fool of Myself

- **Likelihood of Happening:** High
- **Ease of Prevention:** High
- **Is Time a Factor?** No

Alcohol is often heralded as the ideal social lubricant, transforming shy, reserved wallflowers into the life of the party. But like all good things, the secret to alcohol's benefits lies solely in the drinker's ability to use it in moderation. When you overindulge, your drunken antics will certainly leave a lasting impression, just not the kind you were hoping for.

■ Retrace Your Steps

In the uncomfortably bright light of the next morning, your fragmented memories of the night before are unreliable at best. Alcohol can play havoc with your ability to recall important details, so even if you think you behaved yourself it's possible you may have forgotten embarrassing conversations or entire events from the evening's revelry.

Start your detective work with your closest friend or colleague who spent the night out with you. Be upfront and ask if there's anything you might have said or done that might come back to haunt you. Also, go through your cell phone and take note of who you called and texted—or worse, sexted. This might also be a good time to check your credit card statement to see if you really did buy a round for the entire bar, or if you just imagined that part.

■ Own Up to Your Failures

Whether you threw up in your boss's purse or decided to tell your best friend what you really think of his wife, you have a fairly narrow window of time in which to make amends. If possible, frame your actions as a misunderstanding rather than intentional behavior. Research indicates that individuals respond more favorably to an apology where the offense is the result of a mistake.

Good Apology: I'm sorry if I embarrassed you with my boisterous rendition of "Sweet Caroline," but I didn't realize you meant you wanted to try karaoke *someday*, not right that second.

Bad Apology: I'm sorry I stole your wallet, but I was really tired and needed cash for a cab home.

Whatever you do, don't blame your behavior on the booze. Alcohol can do many things, but there isn't a cocktail in existence that can actually take control of your limbs and force a lampshade over your head. You and you alone are responsible for your screwups, and your apologies should reflect that.

Why Booze Leads to Poor Decisions

Alcohol decreases brain activity in the prefrontal cortex, the area normally reserved for higher-level thinking. As a result, you are less likely to consider the future consequences of your actions.

■ Learn the Value of Moderation

If you feel you might have a substance abuse problem, then you should absolutely seek professional help. If, however, this was an isolated incident, then your next night out is the perfect opportunity to demonstrate that you are a responsible adult who went a little overboard, and not an uncontrollable lush. The next time you find yourself out with the same group, make it a point to have one or two drinks and call it a night. While you can certainly abstain entirely, it's possible your refusal to partake will solidify the notion that you can't be trusted around alcohol.

I Forgot My Anniversary

Likelihood of Happening: Moderate
Ease of Prevention: High
Is Time a Factor? Yes

You'd think something that takes place on the same day every year would be easy to remember. Yet according to a British study, as many as 50 percent of men and 37 percent of women can't pinpoint their special day off the top of their head. But it doesn't matter if you don't think it's important enough to make a fuss over if your better half disagrees.

■ Decide How Bad It Is

Hopefully the overlooked anniversary is a realization you are coming to yourself, rather than one your significant other had to point out to you. If that's the case, what do you have time to pull together? Is there still time left in the day to scrape together a romantic evening or run down to the florist to grab some flowers? If it's been a few days, is it possible your partner has forgotten as well?

Another important question to answer is how certain are you of the actual date? You've already forgotten it; you don't want to make things worse by not having a clue when it actually was. If necessary, take a look through your wedding album or do some sleuthing in your e-mail to track down the precise date.

■ Rebuild Burned Bridges

There's really no two ways about it: You screwed up, and you are going to have to make amends. How you do so depends a lot on your partner, your relationship, and whether this is the first time or the eighth time you've done this. Be aware that it's not the lack of a present or a night out that your partner is likely upset about, it's the notion that forgetting the anniversary implies that you don't feel the relationship is important. However you choose to apologize, make sure that you do so in a way that reveals your deep appreciation for your partner. For example, select an activity that you know your significant other enjoys but you rarely get to do together.

■ Deny, Deny, Deny

If honesty isn't your strong suit—and not much time has passed— you may be able to rectify the situation with a teensy-weensy white lie. If confronted about your failure to remember your anniversary, insist that you have a big surprise planned for later in the week and you wanted to catch your partner off-guard. Aside from the dishonesty factor, the only downside to this strategy is you now have to come through on said surprise, so get planning!

I Forgot What's-His-Face's Name

- **Likelihood of Happening:** High
- **Ease of Prevention:** High
- **Is Time a Factor?** No

For some, introductions are no big deal. You say hi, tell each other a little about yourselves, make small talk, and move on with your evening. But for others, meeting new people is an exercise in futility and a stressful reminder that you have as much hope of remembering the person's name as you do memorizing the fourth line of the periodic table.

■ Focus on the Task at Hand

Your brain is bombarded with thousands of pieces of information on any given day, and it does its best to prioritize everything. But you and your brain may have very different opinions when it comes to what is and what is not important. If you want to ensure your new acquaintance's name doesn't go in one ear and exit through the other, you'll have to focus your full attention.

Make a conscious decision to remember the name, as well as key elements about the person. Hair color and style of clothing as well as memorable scars or tattoos can all serve as triggers to help you recall the name later. Repeating the name—either back to the person or quietly to yourself—can also help reinforce to your brain that this bit of information is valuable.

It Can Happen in Seconds

In 1959, two scientists asked volunteers to memorize three random letters and then count backwards from 999 by threes. After just eighteen seconds, almost none of the participants could remember a single one of the three letters.

Other tactics you can employ include rhyming the name, associating the person with a friend with the same name, and combining a characteristic with their name. For example, maybe your boss's husband Rick uses too much hair gel, so you remember him as "Slick Rick."

■ Call for Reinforcements

While you could simply ask old What's-His-Face to repeat his name, a far less embarrassing option is to track down someone else who might be willing to help you out. This could be a friend, coworker, or even a complete stranger who you can introduce to the target and wait patiently for him to offer his name.

Alternatively, you could patrol the outskirts of the conversation and wait for new people to arrive and introduce themselves. Although this method can give the impression that you are eavesdropping, it doesn't require you to admit your failure to have paid attention.

■ Be Tricky

If you are feeling tricky, there are a few tricks you can employ to uncover his name without outing yourself. For example, you could approach him later on in the evening and ask him to tell you his name again. When he offers his first name, insist that you meant his last name to avoid offending him. This one requires moderate acting skill, as you will have to feign confusion when he tells you his first name.

Another option is to ask him to spell his name for you, because you want to connect with him on social media. Be careful though, as this method only works with people with relatively unique names. You will come across as slightly off if you ask someone how to spell "Bob."

Lastly, if all else fails, you can always bring up the tired topic of terrible driver's license photos. If you are lucky, this may prompt him to take his out and allow you a sneak peek at his name. Just try not to forget it this time.

I Have a One-Night Stand with My Coworker

- **Likelihood of Happening:** Low
- **Ease of Prevention:** High
- **Is Time a Factor?** No

Not every sexual encounter needs to be an intimate moment shared between two individuals in a loving, committed relationship. In fact, approximately 44 percent of adults claim to have had a one-night stand at some point in their past. And there's nothing wrong with that—unless, of course, you have to share a cubicle with your casual encounter the next morning.

■ Do Damage Control

Whether you acted on impulse or the open bar at the company holiday party impaired your judgment, you made your bed and now you have to lie in it. Before you do anything else, get started on damage control.

Casual Sex Isn't for Everyone

When it comes to one-night stands, it turns out men are far more likely to enjoy the experience than women. According to a survey of more than 3,000 men and women, 80 percent of the men claimed to have positive feelings about their casual encounters, while only 54 percent of women could make the same assertion.

If you are lucky, the only people who know about your interdepartmental fling are you and the object of your temporary affections. But if any of your coworkers saw you leave together, you can rest assured the rumor mill will be in full force. If you can, isolate anyone whom you think may have reason to be suspicious and consider discussing the situation with him or her. But be cautious. You don't want to out yourself only to discover that your coworkers had no idea.

■ Get Yourselves on the Same Page

Hopefully you have a very good understanding of how you feel about the encounter, but there's a good chance you don't have a clue what the other person is thinking. While it may be uncomfortable—or even embarrassing—to talk about the event, it's important that you both can agree on where to go from here.

Was this a one-time thing, or is there something more the two of you would like to pursue? Do you want to remain friendly in the office, or would you prefer to distance yourselves? Will this encounter negatively affect your ability to work together? If so, do you need to consider alerting HR so you can be moved to different teams?

These are all important questions that can either be dealt with now or ignored until you are forced to deal with them later. Your future self will thank you for handling it now.

■ Weigh Your Career Against Your Choices

It's not at all uncommon for employees to date and even marry someone they met on the job. But if you do choose to continue an ongoing relationship with your one-night stand, you can do serious damage to your career if you aren't careful.

If either of you is in a position of power over the other—like a manager, for example—any serious or casual relationship you enter into could be against corporate policy. Some companies even discourage interoffice dating among employees at the same level. While you might be able to shield yourselves by disclosing your relationship to HR, every company is different. So it's important to be aware of your corporate policies if you decide to extend your one-night stand to a two- or twelve-night stand.

I Step in Dog Poop

Likelihood of Happening: High
Ease of Prevention: Moderate
Is Time a Factor? No

The ASPCA estimates there are as many as 80 million dogs spread throughout the United States, and the average dog poops at least once per day. Even assuming a 99 percent cleanup rate on the part of pet owners—which is extraordinarily generous—that's still approximately 800,000 piles of excrement scattered around the country daily. Like it or not, at some point in your life, you are going to have to deal with the aftermath of stepping in some.

■ Scrape It Off

Once you've determined with relative certainty that you have, in fact, stomped on a dog turd, your primary concern is removing the afflicted shoe without sullying your hands or other shoe. With your fingers placed firmly on the tops of your shoes, you should be able to wiggle your foot out with minimal cross-contamination.

At this point, many desperate individuals will proceed to bang the poop-smeared shoe against a wall or on the ground to dislodge the mess. While moderately effective, there's the unfortunate side effect of spraying dog feces on everything in a six-foot radius—yourself included. Instead, grab a stick, pencil, or other small poking tool and gently scrape off any large clumps. If you are feeling altruistic, track down a plastic shopping bag in which to deposit the aftermath to prevent another passerby from suffering your fate. Don't drive yourself crazy trying to get every last bit. Once you've removed the majority of the poop, place the shoe in a zipper-lock bag and bring it home.

■ Finish the Job

Depending on the style of shoe you were wearing, you could poke and prod for hours and still not remove every last speck of poop. To make the task significantly easier, place your soiled shoe in the freezer for a few hours. Once the excrement hardens, you can use a toothbrush and a toothpick to meticulously scrape out the entirety of the mess.

If you are still not satisfied with the results, there's always the option to throw your shoe in the laundry, assuming it's washer safe. Just keep it clear of the dryer, as the intense heat can warp the shoe. Instead, let it air dry in an open room.

Still uncomfortable with the knowledge that there could be a molecule of fecal matter under your heel? Then it might just be time for a new pair of shoes—and an appointment with a therapist.

I Forgot My Wallet on a Date

- **Likelihood of Happening:** High
- **Ease of Prevention:** High
- **Is Time a Factor?** Yes

Every time you leave the house, you go through the same mental list you've gone through 10,000 times before:

Phone? Check!

Keys? Check!

Wallet? Check!

But every now and then, your brain betrays you and the wallet you swear you brought with you is nowhere to be found. And you can bet your bottom dollar that the fancy restaurant you took your date to isn't going to let you pay your bill with Dentyne Ice.

■ Determine the Nature of the Date

Depending on your situation, forgetting your wallet on a night out might not be the end of the world. If you've been seeing your date for a while, you might already be at a point where you feel comfortable asking her to grab the check this time.

Assuming you normally split the bill 50/50, you may be able to save face by suggesting your date pay for this one while you pay next time. If you do go this route, however, make sure you reciprocate with a meal at a comparable establishment. A trip to Applebee's doesn't exactly carry the same weight as a Michelin three-star restaurant.

But if it's a first date, or you were the one who set the date in the first place, you are probably going to have to solve this dilemma yourself.

■ Use Technology

If the gods of forgetfulness were merciful, chances are good you still have your trusty smartphone in your pocket, and with it a plethora of techy options for settling up with the restaurant. While cash and credit are still king in the foodservice industry, there are a number of restaurants that will accept digital payments from the likes of PayPal, Venmo, Google Wallet, and other popular apps. Depending on where you call home, you might even find a few that accept bitcoin, a form of digital currency.

■ Phone a Friend

If you opted to stay local for your evening out, you might be able to enlist the help of your social network to rescue you from embarrassment. Simply excuse yourself to the bathroom for a minute and use the time to text ten of your closest friends to see if any of them would be willing to come bail you out.

Save the casual acquaintances for a time when you need to borrow a pen. In this case, you need to contact the type of people who would help you move a dead body, no questions asked. It may not seem like a big request at face value, but you are staking your future relationship on whether or not your buddy is actually going to come through on this one.

■ Throw Yourself on the Mercy of the Manager

When all else fails, place your fate in the hands of the manager or owner. You certainly won't be the first person to offer a sob story about a misplaced wallet, so be prepared to present your phone or something else of value as collateral. This can be especially effective if you are a regular and the manager knows you are likely to return.

If that strategy falls flat, your last option—barring coming clean with your date—is to impose on the kindness of strangers and see if an understanding patron can take care of the bill for you with the promise of future repayment. While you may lose a little dignity in the process, it sure beats washing dishes.

My Boss Comes On to Me

— **Likelihood of Happening:** Low
— **Ease of Prevention:** High
— **Is Time a Factor?** No

Office romance is nothing new. A study conducted by the Society for Human Resource Management revealed that approximately 40 percent of workers have dated someone they worked with. While the idea of a secret corporate fling might be enticing, it becomes a bit more complicated when the person vying for your attention also signs your paychecks.

■ Don't Blame Yourself

First and foremost, realize that this isn't your fault. Dressing provocatively, acting friendly and outgoing, smiling frequently, and being attractive are not excuses for unwanted advances. With that out of the way, how you proceed will depend on a number of factors, including the nature of the advances, the relationship you have with your boss, and your company's HR policies.

■ Make It Clear You Aren't Interested

Dealing with a boss who is clearly infatuated with you is a delicate situation. If you go directly to HR, you might jeopardize your boss's career over a simple miscommunication. But fail to act and it could be taken as an endorsement of the behavior. If you feel comfortable being upfront and direct with your boss, your best course of action may be to simply discuss the issue.

Whether your boss makes you uncomfortable with offhand remarks about your appearance or open romantic invitations, you need to make it perfectly clear that you are not interested and that you find the behavior unprofessional. If you feel this truly is a case of misinterpreting signals, then this may be enough to stop the problem in its tracks.

■ Leave a Paper Trail

Assuming your boss doesn't get the hint—or you don't feel comfortable having a one-on-one discussion—your next step is to get an outline of the incident(s) in writing. Send your superior a formal e-mail or letter explaining the conduct that makes you uncomfortable, and request that it cease immediately. Be sure to print out a copy for your own records in case you need to refer to it later.

If that doesn't work, keep detailed records of any past and future transgressions that may occur. These should include dates as well as descriptions of what was said or done by your boss. When it's your word against someone else's, it's always better when your word is written down.

■ Let the Professionals Take Care of It

Unfortunately, you are not the first person to encounter an inappropriate boss. As a result, most human resource departments are fully trained and equipped to handle the situation. When you sit down with HR, be sure to have copies of your notes at the ready. There are a number of different approaches they might take, from mandatory sensitivity training for your boss to outright termination. But if HR fails to resolve the issue to your satisfaction, your only option may be to seek legal counsel.

You also shouldn't feel ashamed or defeated if you choose to seek employment elsewhere rather than deal with the fallout. This just may be a battle you aren't prepared to fight, and you shouldn't feel obligated to.

I've Uncovered an Affair

- **Likelihood of Happening:** Low
- **Ease of Prevention:** Low
- **Is Time a Factor?** No

When it comes to infidelity, the victim is often the last person to know. After the truth does come out and the dust settles, she is often faced with an equally upsetting realization—her friends knew all along. If you do find evidence of a torrid love affair, is it better to bite the bullet and tell the truth or bite your tongue instead?

■ Differentiate Between Proof and Suspicion

Before you dive too deeply down the rabbit hole, keep in mind that you could be setting into motion events that will end your friend's marriage. While this might be the best outcome for everyone involved, you want to be absolutely sure before you start throwing out accusations. Take stock of the situation and consider whether you are grasping at straws or if you might actually be onto something.

■ Consider Confronting the Cheater

Sometimes it's best to hear about infidelity directly from the source—the cheating spouse. If it seems like the issue isn't likely to resolve on its own, perhaps it's time for a heart-to-heart talk with your friend's significant other. Pick a public place for your discussion, and be upfront and honest. Avoid issuing ultimatums, but make it clear how you feel about the situation. Keep in mind that you are not an expert on their relationship, and try hard not to pass judgment.

■ Be Prepared to Lose Your Friend

Should you choose to confront your friend about any marital infidelity, it's likely to end one of two ways:

1. She dumps the cheating spouse and begins the long, emotional process of rebuilding her life.
2. She stays with the cheating spouse and takes her anger out on you for meddling in her personal life.

Even if your suspicions are vindicated, there's still the chance that your relationship with your friend will be forever strained.

■ Be the Messenger

While it's true that the messenger has an unfortunate habit of being shot, you may ultimately have to take that risk. When you do sit your friend down, simply state the facts about the situation and resist the urge to provide unsolicited advice on how you think she should proceed. At the end of the day, the outcome is entirely dependent on your friend and her spouse. Regardless of the decision she comes to, you will need to respect it. While it may be difficult for you if they remain together, take solace in the fact that you had your friend's best interests at heart from the get-go.

I Run Out of Toilet Paper

Likelihood of Happening: Moderate
Ease of Prevention: High
Is Time a Factor? Yes

Haste is both your friend and your enemy when it comes to an urgent bathroom situation. While it can save you from the unpleasantness that might befall you should you fail to make it in time, it can also cause you to overlook one vital piece of information as you frantically sit down on the porcelain throne: Is there any toilet paper?

■ Call for Backup

Depending on your location, this can either be a simple matter of hollering to your spouse in the next room or breaking out your cell phone to text a friend. If you are in a public bathroom, your neighbor in the next stall may be courteous enough to spare a square, or at least alert someone on the outside to your predicament.

But if you find yourself in a solo commode with a line forming outside, you might not have the luxury to wait for reinforcements.

■ Use All of the Buffalo

Our ancestors utilized everything from the skin to the sinew of the animals they hunted, and you must be equally efficient with the items you have at your disposal. The empty toilet-paper roll in front of you might have a few stray scraps of toilet paper that you can harvest to get the job done. Even the cardboard tube itself can be ripped apart and balled together for a makeshift cleaning apparatus—just be sure to wet it first for the sake of comfort.

■ Sacrifice Your Socks

Odds are that you don't have much of an emotional attachment to your socks, which is good considering what you are about to do to them. Your technique is up to you, but keep in mind that efficiency is imperative since you only have two socks. Consider ripping them into strips to maximize their utility.

During flip-flop season, you can also commission your underwear for the unpleasant task at hand, but only use this as a last resort. It's likely your slapdash cleanup job isn't going to be as thorough as usual, and your underwear is a vital line of defense between your rear and the outside world.

If you do use anything that can't be flushed down the toilet to tidy up, do consider the poor individuals using the bathroom after you and adopt a "pack it out" policy. A plastic bag rummaged from the trash should do the trick, or you can even take the whole garbage bag with you.

■ Use Your Last Resort

There's really no delicate way to put this: You're going to have to use your hand. Traditionally the left one, in case you need to shake hands with anyone in the foreseeable future. While it may sound gross, it's really not that unsanitary provided you keep your fingernails free of "debris" and wash them thoroughly when you are finished. The good news is that once you are forced to use your hand once, it will be a cold day in hell before you sit down without assessing the TP situation again.

You've Been Washing Your Hands Wrong

The Center for Disease Control recommends applying soap to wet hands and rubbing them together for at least twenty seconds before rinsing—the average person only spends about six seconds. The CDC recommends humming the "Happy Birthday" song twice to ensure you've lathered long enough.

My Child Is Throwing a Temper Tantrum

Likelihood of Happening: High
Ease of Prevention: Low
Is Time a Factor? No

A well-behaved child is like a rainbow: glorious to behold, but ultimately fleeting. As anyone with a toddler can attest, a pleasant family outing can quickly transform into a lesson in mortified embarrassment if your little angel doesn't get her way.

■ Know the Early Signs

As a parent, you know your kid better than anyone, which means you probably know your child's tantrum triggers. For example, is your child more likely to fly into a rage if he is hungry or sleepy? Is it certain activities or events, like grocery shopping or leaving a toy store without buying anything? You also want to pay attention to subtle—or not so subtle—"tells" that your child may exhibit before a full-on tantrum begins. Maybe her eyes well up or he starts to hold his breath, for example. When you notice these signs, do whatever you need to do to stop the tantrum in its infancy.

■ Pull a Bait-and-Switch

We all like to think our precious darlings are child prodigies, but the truth is it's not that difficult to outwit a three-year-old. If you anticipate a tantrum coming on, try distracting your child with a toy, book, or other special treat. Because a toddler's attention span is relatively short, you may find they forget all about what was making them so upset just a moment ago. Since there's no telling what item might be most effective at any given time, it's best to have a large arsenal of tools on your person at all times. But despite your best efforts, it's always possible that there's nothing you can do to prevent your child from completely losing it.

■ Don't Have Your Own Tantrum

A screaming child flailing around on the floor in a crowded store is enough to force even the most disciplined parents into a rage of their own, but it's important to keep your cool. Keep in mind that your child isn't acting out to spite you, but rather out of frustration with their inability to properly comprehend and express their emotions and desires.

In fact, the best approach is not to react at all. Your crying toddler is well past the point of reasonable discussion, and almost anything you do is only going to make the situation worse. Instead, simply go about your business and wait until she is too emotionally exhausted to continue.

■ Get Out of Dodge

If you find yourself losing a battle of wills with your child, there's no shame in playing your trump card and vacating the premises. A change of location will not only assuage your own embarrassment, but it could even disarm the tantrum outright. However, it's important to note that you should not adopt this strategy if the child's fit is centered on a desire to leave.

I Have to Throw Up in Public

- **Likelihood of Happening:** Moderate
- **Ease of Prevention:** Low
- **Is Time a Factor?** Yes

Depending on the circumstances surrounding the situation you now find yourself in, there are a number of things you should have done differently today. Stayed home in bed instead of going into the office. Thrown away the deli meat with the illegible expiration date rather than using it to make a sandwich. Or perhaps just said "no thanks" instead of "of course I'd like another shot of tequila." But what's done is done, and you have to deal with the consequences.

■ Know the Warning Signs

When your body decides it's time to expel the contents of your stomach, there really isn't much you can do about it. But by paying close attention to your body's signals, you can give yourself time to react and maintain at least some level of dignity. Some warning signs include:

- Heavy salivation
- Pale lips
- Dizziness
- Stomach pain

While these warning signs may appear only seconds before a vomiting episode, this may be enough time to minimize the damage.

■ Consider Your Location

Where you are situated in the world will make all the difference to how you proceed from here. If you are within sprinting distance of a bathroom, garbage can, or sink, your obvious next move is to make a beeline for the nearest receptacle and pray to whichever deities you choose to call upon that you make it in time.

If that's not an option, your next consideration is personal safety. If you are driving a car or operating heavy machinery, for example, your first concern is not to crash or do any major damage. If possible, turn off any machinery or pull your car off to the side of the road before you vomit. If you can't manage to do either, then your only safe option is to tilt your head down slightly and vomit onto your chest. The less you move your head the better, as you'll likely veer in the direction your head is turned.

■ Do a Quick Cost/Benefit Analysis

Assuming you can't make it to a bathroom or garbage can, you need to face an unfortunate fact: Something in your immediate vicinity is going to get thrown up on. Luckily, you do have some control over that, so take a moment to scan your surroundings and do a quick mental evaluation of three things:

1. Which items are too expensive to vomit on?
2. Which items would be a huge pain to cleanse of vomit?
3. Which items are not yours?

If your goal is avoiding embarrassment, then your primary concern at this point is to avoid throwing up on anyone else nearby, or on anyone else's stuff. As for your own things, laptops and any electronics should clearly be avoided, as well as any expensive clothing or carpeting. If you happen to be wearing anything that you wouldn't mind trashing, or you are confident could be easily laundered, then vomiting into your shirt or lap is probably a good option. A cheap purse or bag might also do well, provided there is nothing important contained within.

Be wary of small containers like water bottles or coffee mugs. While they may seem like an ideal choice, they may not be large enough to contain the entire episode's worth of vomit.

My Children Catch Me Having Sex

— **Likelihood of Happening:** Moderate
— **Ease of Prevention:** High
— **Is Time a Factor?** No

If you have biological children—barring artificial insemination— there's a 99.9 percent chance you had sex in order to achieve that. And although we would all like to believe our parents stopped bumping uglies immediately after we were conceived, this simply isn't the case. Parents do continue to have sex, which can pose a bit of a problem in a house full of curious kids.

■ Decide If It's a Nonissue

Before you hold a family meeting, take a moment to consider whether your child is even old enough to comprehend what he just witnessed. If your child is younger than three, then it's unlikely you will even need to acknowledge the incident. If he asks you what was going on, then you can just explain that it's nothing to worry about and save the conversation for a later time. Just make it clear that you and your partner weren't hurting each other, as young children often worry that something violent has occurred.

For older children, who are generally aware of some of the concepts of sex, you may need to be ready for a broader discussion.

■ Have an Open Conversation about Sex

The average age a child is exposed to pornography is 10, so there's a good possibility your kid has at least some concept of what was happening. While it may seem embarrassing, this will be a good chance for you to have an open and honest conversation with them about the realities of sex. Children are naturally very curious, and you should be prepared to answer questions that might make you uncomfortable.

This is also a good opportunity to discuss the notion of privacy. Unless you were having sex somewhere other than your bedroom, it's likely your child wandered in unannounced. While you don't want to use this opportunity to turn the situation around on him, you should stress the importance of knocking before entering a room.

■ Childproof Your Sex Life

Unfortunately, we lack the technology to erase your kid's memories of the time she caught mom and dad doing it, but at least you can prevent it from happening again. If your bedroom doesn't already have locks, install some and turn on the TV or play music to cover any noise. If you have sex toys, films, or anything else of a sexual nature, keep it stored in a locked box in your bedroom.

Don't, however, take this situation as a call to remove all displays of affection from your home. Children look to you when forming their own concept of a healthy relationship, and it's important to demonstrate to them what is and is not appropriate.

I Have Unexpected Guests and My House Is a Mess

— **Likelihood of Happening:** High
— **Ease of Prevention:** High
— **Is Time a Factor?** Yes

There are two states of being for the average home or apartment:

1. "Guest ready," with every knickknack dusted and every random object lovingly placed in its appropriate home.
2. A total disaster area, similar to the aftermath of a low-level earthquake or hurricane.

Of the two, anecdotal evidence suggests that the average home spends 99 percent of its time in the second state.

With that in mind, knowing how to fake it when uninvited guests pop in for a visit is imperative.

■ Hide It Now, Sort It Out Later

Time is ticking, and you simply don't have enough of it to start a philosophical debate on whether the measuring cup belongs with the glassware or in the baking drawer. In the few minutes you have, zip through the main rooms of your house and starting moving clutter anywhere and everywhere you can think of that's out of sight.

Inside closets, underneath beds, or tucked away in trunks—wherever there's space. An unsightly sink full of dirty dishes can become an inscrutable oven full of dirty dishes in a matter of seconds, if you think creatively.

■ Know That "Clean" Is a Relative Term

The directions on your bottle of all-purpose cleaner probably suggest you let it sit a few minutes before you wipe it off. Well, that ain't happening. If it's not visibly dirty, you are going to have to just let it be for now. For any areas that are dusty or grimy, a quick once-over with a static pad or a disinfectant wipe will suffice. When it comes to the bathroom, draw the curtain on the bathtub and focus your attention on the sink and toilet, neither of which need to be clean enough to eat off.

For areas where guests are unlikely to congregate—like bedrooms and offices—simply close the doors and cross your fingers that nobody goes snooping. If you can lock them from the outside, all the better.

■ Channel Your Inner Illusionist

You might not be at "guest ready" levels yet, but you can certainly make it seem like you are. For example, if you have pets and your furniture is covered in pet hair, throw blankets over the cushions to hide the overwhelming abundance of fur. You can also light scented candles to mask any unpleasant odors. Speaking of which, relying on candlelight instead of electric lights will go a long way toward hiding any stray grime that you might have missed in your haste. In addition, anything that can easily be hidden should be. Your windows aren't dirty if nobody can see them through your closely drawn curtains.

■ Embrace the Clutter

If you simply don't have the time—or the motivation—to clean, then your best bet might be to admit defeat and take comfort in the fact that your friends most likely couldn't care less about the stray receipts and dirty bath towels.

Something Gets Stuck "Up There"

├── **Likelihood of Happening:** Low
├── **Ease of Prevention:** High
└── **Is Time a Factor?** No

Part of being a mature adult is recognizing that sex is different for everyone. While standard missionary intercourse may be fine for some folks, others may be drawn to more adventurous sex acts—and there's absolutely nothing wrong with two consenting adults satisfying their sexual curiosities. That said, it's important to realize that things don't always go as planned, and to know how to react when the unexpected— and the uncomfortable—happens.

■ Relax: Both Mentally and Physically

Even if you generally enjoy the sensation of having a foreign body lodged in your anus, chances are pretty good that you aren't too thrilled to have lost track of it. But panicking is pretty much the worst thing you can do, as this will cause your sphincter to contract and make extraction impossible. Instead, take a few deep breaths and try to calm down. As long as the object does not possess any sharp edges and is not likely to break, there's very little to worry about for now.

How Common Is It?

According to a study conducted on two California hospitals, a large urban hospital can expect to see approximately one patient a month presenting with a foreign object lodged in the rectum. Due to the embarrassing nature of transanal extractions, however, the number of cases that go unreported is likely far larger.

■ Leave It for the Professionals

Unless the object in question has not completely retreated into the rectum, you will not be able to remove it safely at home. Any attempts to do so could push the object further in, or worse, cause a life-threatening perforation of the bowel. This is just one instance where you are going to have to swallow your pride and go to the hospital.

Once there, it is important to be honest with your doctor. Save the elaborate story of slipping and falling on your mechanical toothbrush for later—for now, tell the truth. The more information your doctor has about the situation, the easier it will be for her to help alleviate the problem. After discussing the incident with you, the doctor will likely check for any tearing in or around the anus. She may order x-rays to determine the location of the object.

The majority of foreign objects can be removed with relative ease by the doctor without the need for surgery. After administering local anesthetic and possibly other medication to relax the muscles, the doctor will position you in the lithotomy position (on your back with legs in stirrups) and use forceps to grasp the object for removal. If the doctor is unable to remove the object safely, she may recommend surgery.

If you do need a surgical removal, due to the complete relaxation achieved when a patient is under the effects of general anesthesia, a noninvasive extraction may be possible at this point. If not, the surgeon will try various methods of coaxing the object out of the anus before resorting to making an incision in the colon to remove it.

Barring surgical removal, it is likely you will leave the hospital with little more than a sore bum and a mild case of embarrassment. But take comfort in the fact that you are far from the first patient to experience such a dilemma—and you certainly won't be the last.

I Clicked a Not-Safe-for-Work Link at the Office

- **Likelihood of Happening:** Moderate
- **Ease of Prevention:** High
- **Is Time a Factor?** No

The fact that nobody spends their entire workday actually working is one of the worst-kept secrets in the business world. Your employer isn't likely to call you to task for catching up on the news, going over your personal finances, or checking Facebook—unless it gets excessive. But if your personal viewing habits aren't exactly work friendly, there's a serious risk you could lose your job over it.

■ Admit an Accidental Click

Many might question how one could "accidentally" view questionable material at work, but the truth of the matter is it's absolutely possible. Perhaps the text in a forum that said "click here for ten cute pictures of puppies" actually linked to something wildly inappropriate. Maybe your partner sent you a personal image that you opened at work without realizing what it was beforehand.

If it was an accident, your best bet might be to nip the situation in the bud and discuss it with your superior. Many companies keep track of the Internet history of their employees, so it's quite possible that any illicit browsing will be noticed quickly. By taking a proactive approach to the situation, you might be able to explain the event away before you are put on the defensive.

◾ Make the IT Guy Your New Best Friend

If this is not an isolated incident, it's time to start damage control—after you've taken a moment to think about why you can't stop looking at NSFW content at the office. Delete your browser history from your computer and remove any questionable content that you might have stored locally. Then place a call to your company's IT lead and invite him out to lunch.

How you approach this encounter is up to you, but open honesty is usually a good place to start. Explain the situation and ask him about the company's procedures for storing browser history, and if your indiscretions may have been logged. Make sure you are offsite when you have this chat, as your IT professional will feel more comfortable discussing it outside of work.

While you absolutely shouldn't request that he do anything that could jeopardize his own job, you might discover that the company automatically deletes all employee history after a certain timeframe. And who knows, perhaps the IT person will take pity on you and your browsing data will be "automatically deleted" shortly after lunch.

I Clogged Someone Else's Toilet

— **Likelihood of Happening:** Moderate
— **Ease of Prevention:** Moderate
— **Is Time a Factor?** Yes

Normally, a clogged toilet is little more than a minor inconvenience—albeit a gross one. If this happens in your own home when nobody else is around, you have plenty of time to assess the situation and even call a professional for a particularly stubborn clog. But if you are at a crowded gathering with a line of partygoers forming outside the door—or worse, at a date's apartment—then time is a luxury you absolutely don't have.

■ Look Around for Helpful Tools

If a toilet fails to flush on the first attempt, many panicked individuals will try flushing it again. This is a terrible idea, and could result in the toilet overflowing—which is the last thing you want. Instead, locate the shut-off valve underneath the toilet and turn it clockwise to prevent additional water from entering the bowl.

Once the water is turned off, search the bathroom for a plunger. Many homeowners find the plunger to be an unsightly bathroom fixture, so you may have to go looking through closets and in tucked-away corners.

■ Cross Your Fingers and Get to Work

Once you've found the plunger, you might want to run the ceiling fan or even turn on the faucet to mask the sound of your frantic plunging. The fan will also help eliminate any unpleasant odors that may escape. Next, insert the plunger into the bowl and press down slowly to create a tight seal. If the plunger is not completely submerged, add some water from the sink to ensure you aren't forcing air against the clog instead of water.

Once you've created a tight seal, pull up on the plunger to create suction and then push down to force the clog through. This may require several tries, but after a few solid attempts the clog should loosen and you will be able to flush the toilet normally.

▓ Improvise

Discovering a dearth of proper plumbing equipment is certainly panic inducing, but it's not a lost cause. If your host happens to have a wire hanger in the bathroom—or if you can sneak out quickly to grab one from an adjoining bedroom—unravel it to fashion a makeshift plumber's snake and insert it into the bowl to dislodge the clog.

If all you have to work with is soap and water, you have one last ray of hope. Pouring a few squirts of soap into the bowl along with a hefty amount of steaming hot water might be enough to break up the clog and allow you to save face. You will need to give the soapy mixture some time to work, but hopefully after a few minutes the water level will go down and you can start thinking of an excuse for why you were in there for so long.

Index

About the Author

Eric Grzymkowski was born in 1984 in Fair Lawn, New Jersey. He spent his formative years mastering the Nintendo Entertainment System before discovering the Internet in 1995. Since then, he has devoted most of his free time to expanding his knowledge of all things useless and obscure. While working at a mall pet store in 2001, he successfully sold a chihuahua to Olympic gold medalist Oksana Baiul. This remains his greatest achievement to date.